THE CONSTITUTION DECODED

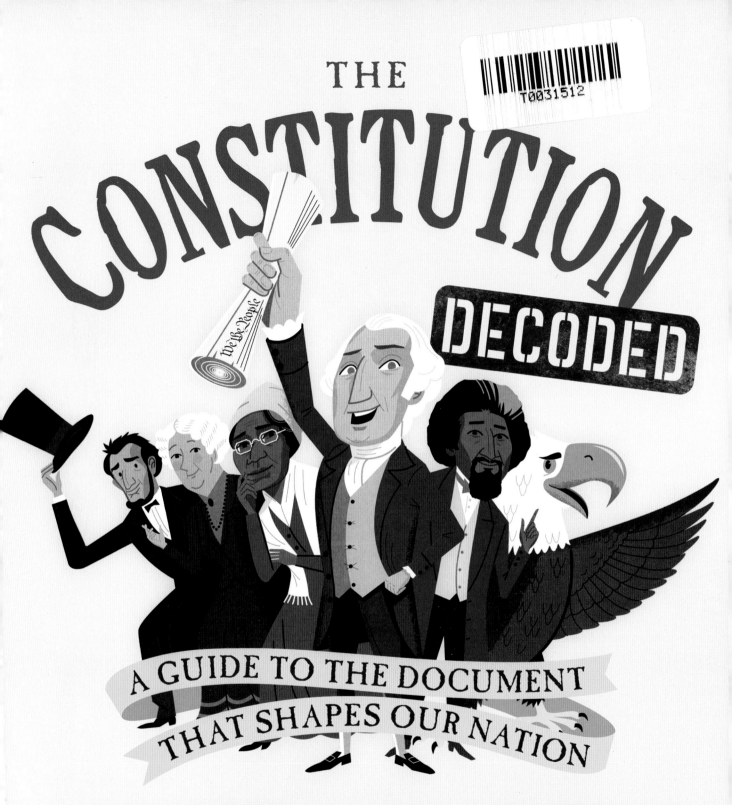

A GUIDE TO THE DOCUMENT THAT SHAPES OUR NATION

BY **KATIE KENNEDY** ★ ILLUSTRATED BY **BEN KIRCHNER**
CONTRIBUTING EDITOR **KERMIT ROOSEVELT**

WORKMAN PUBLISHING COMPANY ★ NEW YORK

T0031512

Library of Congress Cataloging-in-Publication Data is available.
ISBN 978-1-5235-1044-3

Design by John Passineau
Cover illustration by Ben Kirchner

Workman books are available at special discounts when purchased in
bulk for premiums and sales promotions as well as for fund-raising or
educational use. Special editions or book excerpts can also be created to
specification. For details, contact the Special Sales Director at the address
below or send an email to specialmarkets@workman.com.

Workman Publishing Co., Inc.
225 Varick Street
New York, NY 10014-4381

workman.com

WORKMAN is a registered trademark of
Workman Publishing Co., Inc.

Printed in China
First printing July 2020

10 9 8 7 6 5 4 3 2 1

CONTENTS

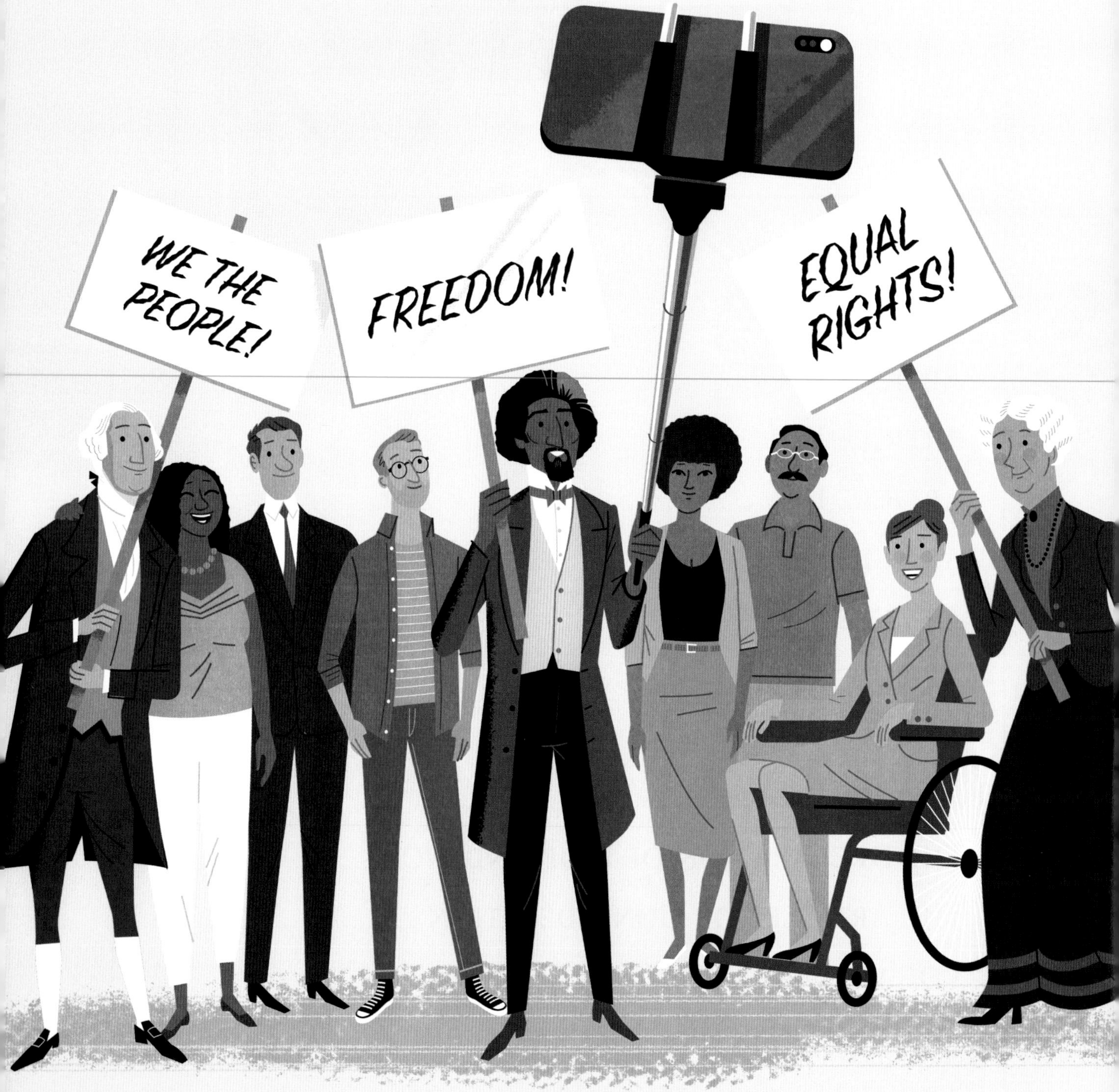
WE THE PEOPLE!
FREEDOM!
EQUAL RIGHTS!

Introduction

In the summer of 1787, fifty-five representatives, or delegates, from the original thirteen states met at Independence Hall in Philadelphia. The colonies had won their independence from Great Britain. They had set up a government that gave power to each state but did not give much power to a national government. After having been ruled by a monarch and having no representation in their government, the states were afraid to put too much power in one governing body. But the government they'd set up under the Articles of Confederation (see page 178) wasn't strong enough to last. The delegates were supposed to tinker with the existing framework. Instead, they wrote a whole new document: the Constitution. The delegates became known as the Framers of the Constitution and included some of the founders of our country, like James Madison, Alexander Hamilton, and George Washington.

The United States Constitution set up a democratic government in which the people elect their representatives. The Constitution was a compromise between large and small states, and it split power between the states and the federal government. It set up three branches of government—the legislative branch (Congress), where laws are made; the executive branch (the president), where laws are enforced; and the judicial branch (judges), where the meaning of a law is determined. Checks and balances keep any one branch from having too much power. The delegates included a way to amend, or change, the document as future generations found it necessary. Today, there are twenty-seven amendments, and they are as fully a part of the Constitution as the original document.

The Constitution is shaped by amendments like the 13th, which ended slavery; the 14th, which protects individuals from state infringement on their rights; and the 19th, which gave women the right to vote. The Bill of Rights, which was added in 1791, is one of the best-known parts of the document. It includes the first ten amendments and guarantees rights like freedom of speech, religion, and the press. The Constitution has been interpreted through Supreme Court cases that have shifted the course of the country, like *Dred Scott v. Sandford*, which said that African Americans couldn't be citizens, and *Korematsu v. United States*, which upheld the order for Japanese Americans to leave their homes on the West Coast during World War II. (*Dred Scott* has been overturned; the Supreme Court has criticized *Korematsu* but has not overturned it.) Other cases helped establish laws and decisions that we continue to live by today. *Griswold v. Connecticut* established a right to privacy. *Gitlow v. New York* said that states have to respect freedom of speech just as the federal government does.

One of the most important parts of the Constitution is the Supremacy Clause. It says that states can't have laws that conflict with the Constitution or those of the federal government, and if there is a disagreement, the state law has to change. People who hold state jobs take an oath to defend the Constitution—even against actions by their own state. Presidents take an oath to defend the Constitution, and if they don't, they can be removed from office. Through every amendment, interpretation, presidency, and crisis, the Constitution remains the law of the land, as it has for almost 250 years.

What can you do to help protect the Constitution? You can learn about the document—how it's organized, what it says, and how it works in practice. After all, it's hard to preserve your freedoms if you don't know what they are.

How to Use This Book:

★ The full and original text of the United States Constitution appears in this book (on the left-hand page) and is side-by-side with an easy-to-follow translation (on the right-hand page). Read the original text on the left until you come to a number in a circle (❶), then find that number on the opposite page to discover what that text means.

★ **Vocabulary words** are bold within the text of the document, and you'll find their definitions in call-out boxes below.

★ **Did You Know?** and **Look Back** boxes offer the story behind the document and explain how or why it was created this way. Sometimes they are accompanied by major figures from history. You can learn more about those people on the following page.

★ **Constitution in Action** boxes show how the document is used in practice and offer further explanations about how our government works.

GEORGE WASHINGTON

Vocabulary

DEMOCRACY—a government run by the people, often through elected representatives

George Washington (1732–1799) commanded the Continental Army in the American Revolution. He was the president of the Constitutional Convention and the first president of the United States.

Harriet Tubman (c. 1821–1913) was born into slavery as Araminta Ross. Despite a head injury that caused her to fall asleep at unpredictable times, she escaped north to freedom—then returned to slave territory repeatedly to lead other slaves to freedom. She spied for the Union army during the Civil War and was a women's rights activist in her later years.

Dred Scott (1799–1858) was a slave who tried to sue for his freedom. He was unsuccessful, and his case, *Dred Scott v. Sandford*, was one of the factors that set the United States on the path to the Civil War.

James Madison (1751–1836) was a delegate from Virginia to the Constitutional Convention. He had a major role in writing the Constitution and getting it ratified by the states. He became the fourth president of the United States.

INTRODUCTION

Frederick Douglass (1818–1895) was born a slave and escaped to freedom. He was a powerful abolitionist, or anti-slavery, speaker.

Richard Oakes (1942–1972) was a Mohawk who advocated for Native American rights. Oakes helped get universities to offer Native American studies programs. In 1969, he and other activists occupied Alcatraz Island in San Francisco Bay to increase awareness of problems facing Native Americans. He was killed in 1972.

Martin Luther King Jr. (1929–1968) was a Baptist minister and a leader of the civil rights movement in the 1950s and '60s. He advocated for nonviolent protest and won a Nobel Peace Prize. He was assassinated in 1968.

Elizabeth Cady Stanton (1815–1902) was a women's rights and women's suffrage (vote) activist, as well as an abolitionist. She was one of the organizers of the Seneca Falls Convention (1848), which is often seen as the beginning of the women's rights movement.

Sojourner Truth (c. 1797–1883) was an abolitionist and women's rights activist. She was born into slavery as Isabella Baumfree to a Dutch-speaking family in New York. She is best known for her "Ain't I a Woman?" speech.

PREAMBLE ❶

We the People of the United States, in Order to form a more perfect Union ❷, establish Justice ❸, insure domestic Tranquility ❹, provide for the common defence ❺, promote the general Welfare ❻, and secure the Blessings of Liberty to ourselves and our Posterity ❼, do ordain and establish this **Constitution** for the United States of America ❽.

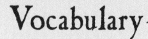

At the time the Constitution was written, it was meant to govern the original thirteen states: Delaware, Pennsylvania, New Jersey, Georgia, Connecticut, Massachusetts, Maryland, South Carolina, New Hampshire, Virginia, New York, North Carolina, and Rhode Island. These were the colonies that fought the British for their independence.

Today, the Constitution applies to the whole country, including places that are not states, like US territories (Puerto Rico, the US Virgin Islands, Guam, American Samoa, Northern Mariana Islands) and the District of Columbia.

Vocabulary

CONSTITUTION—a document that establishes the basic principles of a government, how it will operate, and the rights of its citizens

1. The Preamble is the introduction to the United States Constitution and defines the goals for setting up a new government.

2. We the people of the United States, to make the states into a single country,

3. make things fair,

4. keep the peace at home,

5. defend ourselves from invasion,

6. advance the public well-being,

7. and guarantee our freedom now and for future generations,

8. do create this structure of government for the United States of America.

United States

CONSTITUTION IN ACTION

WHO ARE "THE PEOPLE"?

The Framers of the Constitution used the phrase "We the People" in the Preamble, but the new government didn't represent everyone in the country at the time or later. Slavery continued to exist in many states for seventy-six years after the Constitution went into effect in 1789, and it prevented slaves—who were considered to be property—from having any rights. In 1857, the Supreme Court said that Blacks couldn't become US citizens. The 14th Amendment changed that in 1868. Black men finally got the right to vote in 1870, but they weren't able to use that right until the Voting Rights Act was passed in 1965. Women weren't guaranteed the right to vote until 1920. Native Americans, who lived in what became the United States before White and Black people arrived, experienced sharp discrimination and violence. And some immigrants, like the Chinese and Irish, and gay and transgender people have been kept from fully using their constitutional rights.

Article I.

The Framers expected the legislature, which makes the laws, to be the most important branch of government, so they put it first in the Constitution. Article I sets up the national legislature, including its structure, who can run for office, how laws are made, and the powers that Congress does and does not have.

SECTION 1.

All legislative Powers herein granted shall be vested in a **Congress** of the United States **1**, which shall consist of a **Senate** and **House of Representatives** **2**.

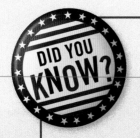

DID YOU KNOW?

The original thirteen states grew out of separate colonies founded by different people at different times. They were governed by the Articles of Confederation (in effect from 1781 to 1789), which treated them like separate countries. The national legislature only had the powers specifically listed in the Articles. It couldn't make laws that affected individuals. There was no president and there were no national courts.

The Framers of the Constitution had to find a balance between the states and the national government. They ultimately rejected the approach in the Articles of Confederation and made it broader. The Constitution gives the United States a federal system. This means that power is shared by the national and state governments. Both levels have some powers that the other doesn't, although the national government is much more powerful. State and local governments have the power to create laws to run the state or town. Those laws cannot conflict with the laws of the federal government (see pages 12–13 for examples).

Vocabulary

CONGRESS—the lawmaking body, or legislature, which passes laws that apply to the whole country

SENATE—the upper chamber, or part, of Congress. It is made up of one hundred senators—two from each state. Senators serve longer terms than members of the House of Representatives. The Senate is the "upper" chamber because originally senators were elected by state legislatures. The Framers thought this would distance senators from the people and provide stability to Congress.

HOUSE OF REPRESENTATIVES—the lower chamber, or part, of Congress, which has 435 members who are divided among the states based on their populations. Representatives serve shorter terms than senators. The House is the "lower" chamber because representatives have always been elected directly by the people. The Framers thought the House would be more connected to the people and their needs.

1 All the power to make laws under the Constitution belongs to the Congress of the United States,

2 which will be made up of the Senate and the House of Representatives.

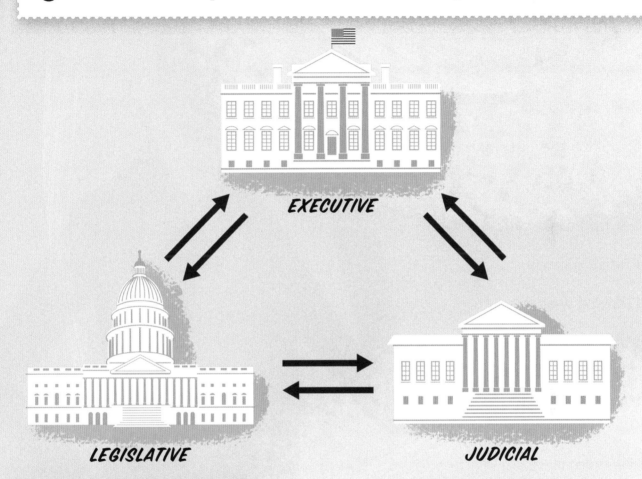

EXECUTIVE

LEGISLATIVE

JUDICIAL

CONSTITUTION IN ACTION

SEPARATION OF POWERS AND CHECKS AND BALANCES

Separation of powers and checks and balances are essential to the functioning of the United States government. The Constitution created three branches of government that would share the responsibility of running the country. Article I sets up the legislature, where the laws are made. Article II creates the executive branch and the office of the president, who enforces the laws.

Article III talks about the judicial system, or courts, where judges decide what the laws mean.

"Separation of powers" means that no one branch of government has all the power. Because of this, one branch usually can't achieve its goals alone.

"Checks and balances" means that the three branches of government check one another's actions. If one branch fails to check another the way it's supposed to, the government would be out of balance and a small group of people could take control. That could be dangerous for democracy.

EXAMPLES OF POWERS ASSIGNED TO

THE FEDERAL GOVERNMENT CAN:

Make tax laws and collect taxes

Borrow money

Regulate the national economy

Manufacture money

Set up a post office system

Punish pirates

Declare war

Raise an army and navy

Make all the laws for Washington, DC, and places that aren't states

Make treaties

Appoint federal judges

Bring Congress into session

Count the population

Hold trials for violations of federal law

Interpret the Constitution

Create national parks

FEDERAL, STATE, AND LOCAL GOVERNMENTS

STATE GOVERNMENTS CAN:

Make tax laws and collect taxes

Issue licenses (such as driver's or fishing licenses)

Hold elections

Write laws that apply only to that state

Ratify amendments to the US Constitution

Hold trials for violations of state laws

Make the state budget

Have a police force

Set up local governments

LOCAL GOVERNMENTS CAN:

Make tax laws and collect taxes

Set up police and fire departments

Run a bus system

Fix sewers

Arrange for snow removal

Start libraries

SECTION 2.

The House of Representatives shall be composed of Members chosen every second Year by the People of the several States **1**, and the **Electors** in each State shall have the Qualifications requisite for Electors of the most numerous Branch of the **State Legislature 2**.

No Person shall be a Representative who shall not have attained to the Age of twenty five Years, and been seven Years a Citizen of the United States, and who shall not, when elected, be an Inhabitant of that State in which he shall be chosen **3**.

DID YOU KNOW?

The Framers couldn't decide whether to give every state the same number of representatives. Big states, like Virginia, wanted more representation because more people lived there. Small states, like Rhode Island, wanted representation to be equal for all states. The Framers came to what is known as the Great Compromise. They created a House of Representatives, where larger states got more votes. The number of representatives is based on a state's population. And they created a Senate, where each state had the same number of votes. Each state gets two senators.

Vocabulary

ELECTORS—voters

STATE LEGISLATURE—the lawmaking body for a state, which can write laws affecting only that state

TRANSLATION

1. The House of Representatives is made up of members who serve two-year terms and are elected by the people of each state,

2. and people are qualified to vote for members of the House of Representatives if they can vote for their state's lawmaking body that has the most members.

3. No one can be a member of the House of Representatives unless they're at least twenty-five years old, have been a US citizen for at least seven years, and live in the state that they'll represent at the time of the election.

ORIGINAL TEXT

[Representatives and **direct Taxes** shall be apportioned among the several States which may be included within this Union, according to their respective Numbers **4**, which shall be determined by adding to the whole Number of free Persons **5**, including those bound to Service for a Term of Years **6**, and excluding Indians not taxed **7**, three fifths of all other Persons **8**.] *(Note: The previous sentence was changed by the 14th Amendment, Section 2 **9**.)*

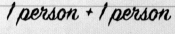

1 person + 1 person = 2 people

3/5 person + 3/5 person = 1 and 1/5 people

Vocabulary

DIRECT TAXES—taxes on people or property rather than activities or transactions

INDENTURED SERVANTS—people who signed a contract to work for a set number of years in exchange for food and shelter, and sometimes for passage to America

TAXES—money paid to the government from people's wages and companies' profits. Taxes are also added to the cost of things that people buy.

TRANSLATION

(4) [The number of representatives in Congress and the amount of taxes owed by individuals will be divided between the states according to their populations,

(5) which will be figured out by counting all free men, women, and children,

(6) including **indentured servants**,

(7) not counting untaxed Native Americans,

(8) and counting each slave as three-fifths of a person.]

(9) Note: Bracketed text changed by the 14th Amendment, Section 2.* See page 134.

Changed so that all inhabitants are counted as a full person.

The founders of the United States fought for their freedom and often wrote about liberty. The Declaration of Independence contains the famous line, "We hold these truths to be self-evident, that all men are created equal, that they are endowed by their Creator with certain unalienable Rights, that among these are Life, Liberty, and the pursuit of Happiness."

There was always a tension between this talk of liberty and the existence of slavery in America. Many of the Framers of the Constitution knew it looked bad to demand liberty for themselves while denying it to other people. But they didn't end the international slave trade or free the slaves who were already in the country. When they debated how to decide on representation in Congress, slave-holding and free states disagreed. Because states with more people get more representatives in the House, slave states wanted to count slaves even though their interests wouldn't be represented. Other states said that it was unfair to count them at all since slave owners claimed their slaves were property. People in free states thought slave owners shouldn't get more power in government because they owned slaves. Finally they agreed to the Three-Fifths Compromise: For purposes of representation, each slave counted as three-fifths of a person. This stood until the 13th Amendment (1865) banned slavery and the 14th Amendment (1868) made freed slaves citizens and said representation would be based on the "whole number of persons in each State" reduced by the number of male citizens over twenty-one who were not allowed to vote.

HARRIET TUBMAN

ORIGINAL TEXT

The actual **Enumeration** shall be made within three Years after the first Meeting of the Congress of the United States ❿, and within every subsequent Term of ten Years, in such Manner as they shall by Law direct ⓫. The Number of Representatives shall not exceed one for every thirty Thousand, but each State shall have at Least one Representative ⓬; and until such enumeration shall be made, the State of New Hampshire shall be entitled to **chuse** three, Massachusetts eight, Rhode-Island and Providence Plantations one, Connecticut five, New-York six, New Jersey four, Pennsylvania eight, Delaware one, Maryland six, Virginia ten, North Carolina five, South Carolina five, and Georgia three ⓭. When vacancies happen in the Representation from any State, the Executive Authority thereof shall issue Writs of Election to fill such Vacancies ⓮.

The House of Representatives shall chuse their Speaker and other Officers ⓯; and shall have the sole Power of **Impeachment** ⓰.

CONSTITUTION IN ACTION

REDISTRICTING

A census, or count of the population, is taken every ten years. This helps determine a state's representation in the House and how a state draws the lines for its voting districts. The number of representatives a state gets in the House is based on its population. If a state's population goes up, it might get more representatives. If its population goes down, it could lose some.

State legislatures draw the lines for electoral districts. These districts determine where you vote. When there's a census, a state can draw new district lines.

If the lines are drawn in a complicated way in order to make the vote come out a certain way, that's called "gerrymandering." Gerrymandering hurts democracy because it makes some people's votes count more than others. It's also a way to reduce the voting power of particular groups, usually based on race or political affiliation.

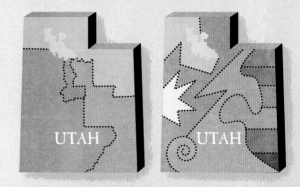

TRANSLATION

10 The population will be counted within three years of Congress's first meeting,

11 and will be counted every ten years, as Congress directs.

12 There won't be more than one representative for every thirty thousand people, but every state will have at least one representative.

13 Until the first count is taken, the number of representatives will be: New Hampshire, 3; Massachusetts, 8; Rhode Island and Providence Plantations, 1; Connecticut, 5; New York, 6; New Jersey, 4; Pennsylvania, 8; Delaware, 1; Maryland, 6; Virginia, 10; North Carolina, 5; South Carolina, 5; and Georgia, 3.

14 When a state has an empty seat in the House of Representatives, its governor will call for an election to fill the spot.

15 The House of Representatives will choose a Speaker of the House and other officers.

16 Only the House can impeach federal officials.

Vocabulary

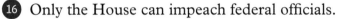

ENUMERATION—a count, or census. A census counts the entire population of the country.

CHUSE—choose (The Constitution has some spellings we don't use anymore—and also some random capitalization and typos!)

IMPEACHMENT—charging an official, like the president, the vice president, or a Supreme Court justice, with treason, bribery, or misuse of government power

SECTION 3.

1. The Senate of the United States shall be composed of two Senators from each State, [chosen by the Legislature thereof ❶,] (*Note: changed by the 17th Amendment* ❷) for six Years; and each Senator shall have one Vote ❸.

2. Immediately after they shall be assembled in Consequence of the first Election, they shall be divided as equally as may be into three Classes ❹. The Seats of the Senators of the first Class shall be vacated at the Expiration of the second Year, of the second Class at the Expiration of the fourth Year, and of the third Class at the Expiration of the sixth Year ❺, so that one third may be chosen every second Year ❻; [and if Vacancies happen by Resignation, or otherwise, during the Recess of the Legislature of any State, the Executive thereof may make temporary Appointments until the next Meeting of the Legislature, which shall then fill such Vacancies ❼.] *(Note: Bracketed text was changed by the 17th Amendment* ❽*.)*

DID YOU KNOW?

All senators serve six-year terms. But if all the new senators in the very first Congress had served six years, they'd all have left office at the same time. The Framers didn't want every senator to be new after each election. After all, the Senate was the chamber that was supposed to provide stable leadership for the government. So they wrote instructions in the Constitution that when the Senate met for the first time, it would divide senators into three classes. The first class's term would end after only two years, the second class's after four years, and the third class would stay for the full six-year term. That set up a staggered system where one-third of the senators leave office every two years. You can look up your state's two senators and find out which class they're in because the system is still in place today.

TRANSLATION

1 The Senate will have two senators from each state [chosen by that state's legislature]

2 Note: Bracketed text changed by the 17th Amendment.* See page 142.

Changed who elects senators—from the state to the people!

3 who serve six-year terms, and each senator has one vote.

4 As soon as they meet after the first election, they'll be divided into three groups.

5 The first group's term will end after two years, the second group's after four years, and the third group's after the full six years,

6 so that one-third of the senators are elected every two years.

7 [If a seat becomes empty because a senator quits, or for any reason, while a state legislature isn't meeting, that state's governor can pick someone to be the senator temporarily, until the state legislature meets again and can choose someone.]

8 Note: Bracketed text changed by the 17th Amendment.* See page 142.

Changed so that senators are elected by the people and not by the state legislatures. (The governor can still choose a temporary replacement if needed.)

3. No Person shall be a Senator who shall not have attained to the Age of thirty Years, and been nine Years a Citizen of the United States, and who shall not, when elected, be an Inhabitant of that State for which he shall be chosen **9**.

4. The Vice President of the United States shall be President of the Senate, but shall have no Vote, unless they be equally divided **10**.

5. The Senate shall chuse their other Officers, and also a **President pro tempore**, in the Absence of the Vice President, or when he shall exercise the Office of President of the United States **11**.

6. The Senate shall have the sole Power to try all Impeachments **12**. When sitting for that Purpose, they shall be on **Oath or Affirmation 13**. When the President of the United States is tried, the **Chief Justice** shall preside **14**: And no Person shall be convicted without the Concurrence of two thirds of the Members present **15**.

7. Judgment in Cases of Impeachment shall not extend further than to removal from Office, and disqualification to hold and enjoy any Office of honor, Trust or Profit under the United States **16**: but the Party convicted shall nevertheless be liable and subject to **Indictment**, Trial, Judgment and Punishment, according to Law **17**.

ARTICLE I. ★ SECTION 3. (continued)

Vocabulary

PRESIDENT PRO TEMPORE—a senator who is in charge of the Senate when the vice president of the United States isn't there

OATH OR AFFIRMATION—An oath is a promise to tell the truth. An affirmation is saying that you'll tell the truth without swearing it. (Some people have religious objections to swearing an oath.)

CHIEF JUSTICE—the head of the Supreme Court, who is the top-ranking judge in the country

INDICTMENT—an official charge that someone has committed a crime

9　No one can be a senator unless they're at least thirty years old, have been a citizen for at least nine years, and live in the state they'll represent at the time of the election.

10　The vice president of the United States is the president of the Senate but doesn't vote unless the senators' votes are tied.

11　The Senate chooses its other officers, including a president pro tempore, who acts as president of the Senate when the US vice president is gone or is acting as president.

12　Only the Senate can hold impeachment trials.

13　When they're trying an impeachment case, senators take an oath.

14　When the US president is on trial in an impeachment, the chief justice of the Supreme Court is in charge of the trial.

15　And no one will be found guilty unless two-thirds of the senators agree.

16　If impeached and found guilty by the Senate, a person will only be punished by losing their government job, and not being allowed to hold any other office again in the federal government,

17　but that person can still be charged, tried, and punished for their actions through the justice system.

IMPEACHMENT

CHIEF JUSTICE

PRESIDENT PRO TEMPORE

SECTION 4.

1. The Times, Places and Manner of holding Elections for Senators and Representatives, shall be prescribed in each State by the Legislature thereof ❶; but the Congress may at any time by Law make or alter such Regulations, except as to the Places of chusing Senators ❷.

2. The Congress shall assemble at least once in every Year, and such Meeting shall be ❸ [on the first Monday in December ❹,] *(Note: Bracketed text was changed by the 20th Amendment, section 2 ❺)* unless they shall by Law appoint a different Day ❻.

DID YOU KNOW?

The English king could stop the English legislature from working whenever he wanted to. In fact, in the 1600s, King Charles I didn't let Parliament meet for eleven years. The Framers wanted to be sure that Congress would meet regularly and not be controlled by a king or president. They added a specific date to the Constitution to make sure that Congress would meet every year.

1. The state legislature in each state will set the time, place, and way of holding elections for senators and representatives,

2. but Congress has the authority to change these rules at any time except for the place where senators are elected.

3. Congress will meet at least once every year, and that meeting will be held

4. [on the first Monday in December,]

5. Note: Bracketed text changed by the 20th Amendment, Section 2.★ See page 148.
   ★*Changed so that the meeting date is January 3. Happy New Year!*

6. unless they make a law to change the day.

CONSTITUTION IN ACTION

CONGRESSIONAL SESSIONS

When Congress meets, it is "in session." Most of the time, each Congress has two sessions. The first session starts in January (as required by the 20th Amendment) and ends in December, and the second runs for the same period the next year. After two years, a new Congress is elected. (It's still called a "new" Congress even if some of its members have been reelected.)

Congress may take recesses, or breaks, during a session. And it can hold extra sessions. If it meets again after stopping, it's called a "special session." If the president calls Congress together—for example, if something comes up that needs attention—it's called an "extraordinary session." When the House and Senate meet together for official business, it's called a "joint session." But if they're meeting unofficially— for example, to hear someone speak—it's called a "joint meeting."

HOUSE SPEAKER

TYPES OF CONGRESSIONAL MEETINGS

MEETINGS	DESCRIPTION	PARTIES INVOLVED
Session	A regular, scheduled meeting of Congress	House and Senate together
Special session	Unscheduled meeting	House and/or Senate
Extraordinary session	President calls Congress into an unscheduled session	House and/or Senate (the Senate has been called back more often than the House)
Joint session	Unscheduled meeting	House and Senate together
Joint meeting	Unscheduled, unofficial meeting	House and Senate together

EXAMPLES

Regular annual meeting of Congress

Franklin Roosevelt called Congress into special session when WWII began in September 1939 to declare American neutrality.

Abraham Lincoln called Congress into extraordinary session on July 4, 1861, to deal with states seceding from, or leaving, the Union.

The president usually delivers the State of the Union address to a joint session of Congress.

In 1941, British Prime Minister Winston Churchill spoke to Congress in a joint meeting, and in 1951, General Douglas MacArthur gave a farewell address to Congress after President Harry Truman fired him.

SECTION 5.

Each House shall be the Judge of the Elections, Returns and Qualifications of its own Members ❶, and a **Majority** of each shall constitute a **Quorum** to do Business ❷; but a smaller Number may adjourn from day to day ❸, and may be authorized to compel the Attendance of absent Members, in such Manner, and under such Penalties as each House may provide ❹.

Each House may determine the Rules of its Proceedings, punish its Members for disorderly Behaviour, and, with the Concurrence of two thirds, expel a Member ❺.

Each House shall keep a Journal of its Proceedings, and from time to time publish the same, excepting such Parts as may in their Judgment require Secrecy ❻; and the Yeas and Nays of the Members of either House on any question shall, at the Desire of one fifth of those Present, be entered on the Journal ❼.

Neither House, during the Session of Congress, shall, without the Consent of the other, adjourn for more than three days ❽, nor to any other Place than that in which the two Houses shall be sitting ❾.

DID YOU KNOW?

The Constitutional Convention kept no official record of its meetings. But when the Framers set up Congress, the convention delegates wanted to be sure that the official proceedings were recorded and the people could find out what Congress was doing. Each chamber's journal records votes and other actions it takes.

Vocabulary

MAJORITY—more than half

QUORUM—the minimum number of members who need to be present in the House or Senate so its work will be official

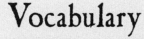

1 The House of Representatives and the Senate are each in charge of judging the elections, results, and qualifications of their own members,

2 and a majority of each chamber counts as a quorum to hold votes;

3 but less than a majority of the whole chamber can decide to stop work for the day,

4 and less than a majority of the whole chamber can force absent members to show up in whatever way and with whatever penalty each chamber decides on.

5 The House of Representatives and the Senate decide on their own rules for doing their business, can discipline members for acting badly, and, if two-thirds of the members agree, can kick somebody out.

6 The House of Representatives and the Senate each keep a journal of what they say and do and publish it occasionally, except for parts that they decide need to stay private.

7 The "yes" and "no" votes of members in either chamber on any question will be entered in the journal if one-fifth of the members present agree.

8 While Congress is in session, neither the House of Representatives nor the Senate can, without the other's permission, stop meeting for more than three days,

9 and they can't move to a different place.

CONSTITUTION IN ACTION

CONGRESS IN CHARGE OF ITS OWN

The House and Senate are in charge of their own chambers. Members of Congress can only be expelled, or kicked out, if two-thirds of the chamber agree. Members can be expelled for any reason, not necessarily because they have committed a crime.

Congress can also discipline members for bad behavior. In 1798, Representative Roger Griswold taunted Representative Matthew Lyon, who then spat tobacco juice on him. Lyon had to write a letter of apology. Later, the two swung at each other with a cane and a set of fireplace tongs, and the House ordered both men to keep the peace.

ORIGINAL TEXT

SECTION 6.

[The Senators and Representatives shall receive a Compensation for their Services, to be ascertained by Law, and paid out of the Treasury of the United States ❶.] *(Note: The preceding words were modified by the 27th Amendment ❷.)* They shall in all Cases, except **Treason**, **Felony** and Breach of the Peace, be privileged from Arrest during their Attendance at the Session of their respective Houses, and in going to and returning from the same ❸; and for any Speech or Debate in either House, they shall not be questioned in any other Place ❹.

No Senator or Representative shall, during the Time for which he was elected, be appointed to any civil Office under the Authority of the United States ❺, which shall have been created, or the **Emoluments** whereof shall have been encreased during such time ❻; and no Person holding any Office under the United States, shall be a Member of either House during his Continuance in Office ❼.

DID YOU KNOW?

The Constitution protects members of Congress from being arrested, except for serious crimes, while they're working or on the way to or from work. And they can't be punished in any way for anything said in a speech to Congress or during a debate there.

Vocabulary

TREASON—making war against the government or helping its enemies

FELONY—a serious crime. Felonies are sometimes violent and are bigger crimes than misdemeanors. A person convicted of a felony can go to jail for more than one year.

EMOLUMENTS—money or items of value

TRANSLATION

1. [Legislators are paid for their work, and their salaries are set by law and paid by the US Treasury.]

2. Note: Bracketed text changed by the 27th Amendment.* See page 168.

   Changed to prevent Congress from voting for a pay raise for itself. All raises begin with the next session of Congress.

3. Except in cases of treason, felonies, or public disturbance, legislators can't be arrested at work or while traveling there or back,

4. and they can't be punished for their speeches or debates anyplace else, either.

5. During the term they were elected, senators and representatives can't hold another government job

6. that was created or had its pay raised during that time,

7. and no one can be a member of Congress while holding any other government job.

ORIGINAL TEXT

SECTION 7.

All **Bills** for raising **Revenue** shall originate in the House of Representatives ❶; but the Senate may propose or concur with Amendments as on other Bills ❷.

Every Bill which shall have passed the House of Representatives and the Senate, shall, before it become a Law, be presented to the President of the United States ❸; If he approve he shall sign it, but if not he shall return it, with his Objections to that House in which it shall have originated, who shall enter the Objections at large on their Journal, and proceed to reconsider it ❹. If after such Reconsideration two thirds of that House shall agree to pass the Bill, it shall be sent, together with the Objections, to the other House, by which it shall likewise be reconsidered, and if approved by two thirds of that House, it shall become a Law ❺. But in all such Cases the Votes of both Houses shall be determined by Yeas and Nays, and the Names of the Persons voting for and against the Bill shall be entered on the Journal of each House respectively ❻.

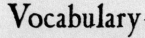

Congress passes a lot of laws. But the Constitution is a higher kind of law. It sets up the government and explains how it will work. It gives Congress the power to pass laws that help the country run. The only things that get added to the Constitution are amendments. Congress passes them and submits them to the states for ratification, or agreement. If enough states ratify an amendment, it becomes part of the Constitution. Amendments are rare—only twenty-seven have ever been ratified.

Vocabulary

BILLS—written drafts of laws

REVENUE—income; for example, money coming to the government from people paying taxes

TRANSLATION

1. All tax bills will start in the House of Representatives,

2. but the Senate can suggest changes, as it does with other bills, and it has to agree to tax and spending bills for them to become law.

3. Every bill that is approved by both the House of Representatives and the Senate goes to the president before it becomes a law.

4. If the president signs a bill, it becomes a law. But if the president doesn't like a bill, he can send it back to the chamber where it started and say what he didn't like about it. The legislators will write what the president thought was wrong in their journal and then talk about the bill again.

5. If two-thirds of that chamber still wants to pass the bill after thinking it over again, the bill will be sent along with the president's concerns to the other chamber. They'll talk about it, and if two-thirds of the other chamber approves it, too, it will become law.

6. These votes are written down in the journal of each chamber, including the names of the people voting for and against the bill.

ORIGINAL TEXT

If any Bill shall not be returned by the President within ten Days (Sundays excepted) after it shall have been presented to him, the Same shall be a Law, in like Manner as if he had signed it **7**, unless the Congress by their Adjournment prevent its Return, in which Case it shall not be a Law **8**.

Every **Order**, **Resolution**, or Vote to which the Concurrence of the Senate and House of Representatives may be necessary (except on a question of Adjournment) shall be presented to the President of the United States **9**; and before the Same shall take Effect, shall be approved by him **10**, or being disapproved by him, shall be repassed by two thirds of the Senate and House of Representatives, according to the Rules and Limitations prescribed in the Case of a Bill **11**.

CONSTITUTION IN ACTION

HOW BILLS BECOME LAWS

A bill becomes a law when it has been passed by both the House of Representatives and the Senate and the president has signed it. If the president refuses to sign, it's called a "veto." Congress can still pass the bill if two-thirds of the members of both chambers vote to approve it.

Vocabulary

ORDER—instruction given by someone in charge; a command

RESOLUTION—a formal decision or proposal voted on by a legislature

TRANSLATION

7 If the president doesn't send a bill back to Congress within ten days after he gets it (not including Sundays), it becomes a law just as if he had signed it,

8 unless the president can't return the bill because Congress is no longer in session; then it doesn't become a law.

9 All the orders, resolutions, and votes that require agreement of the House and Senate, except for votes to stop work, go to the president,

10 and before any of them become a law, the president has to approve them,

11 but if he doesn't approve them, they can be passed by two-thirds of both chambers, according to the rules they've set up.

SECTION 8.

The Congress shall have Power To lay and collect Taxes, **Duties**, **Imposts** and **Excises** ❶, to pay the Debts and provide for the common Defence and general Welfare of the United States ❷; but all Duties, Imposts and Excises shall be uniform throughout the United States ❸;

To borrow money on the credit of the United States ❹;

To regulate Commerce with foreign Nations, and among the several States, and with the Indian Tribes ❺;

To establish an uniform Rule of **Naturalization** ❻, and uniform Laws on the subject of Bankruptcies throughout the United States ❼;

To coin Money, regulate the Value thereof, and of foreign Coin ❽, and fix the Standard of Weights and Measures ❾;

To provide for the Punishment of counterfeiting the Securities and current Coin of the United States ❿;

To establish Post Offices and post Roads ⓫;

To promote the Progress of Science and useful Arts, by securing for limited Times to Authors and Inventors the exclusive Right to their respective Writings and Discoveries ⓬;

DID YOU KNOW?

Article I, Section 8 is the Enumerated Powers Clause. This is the list of powers specifically given to Congress by the Constitution. When the Framers decided to move away from the Articles of Confederation, which gave the federal government very little power, to a constitution that would provide for a stronger national government, they specifically listed some powers to make sure people understood the government's authority.

The ability to set up postal roads and post offices may be the least interesting of the enumerated powers, but it started the national system of roads and bridges that now covers thousands of miles. In addition, the post office helped unify the country. Sometimes the only federal officials in a town or county were postal officers.

ARTICLE I. ★ SECTION 8.

TRANSLATION

1. Congress has the power to write tax bills and collect taxes, duties, imposts, and excises

2. to pay US debts, defend the country, and help the people be successful,

3. but all duties, imposts, and excises have to be the same from state to state;

4. to borrow money for the federal government on the promise that it will repay it;

5. to control our interactions with other countries, as well as between the states and with Native American nations;

6. to make rules on becoming a citizen that will be the same in all states

7. and laws to deal with getting out of debt that will be the same in all states;

8. to manufacture money and decide how much it's worth, and what it's worth compared to foreign money,

9. and to decide on consistent units to measure and weigh goods;

10. to decide on punishments for making fake money;

11. to create post offices and roads for use in delivering the mail;

12. to help science and the arts by letting authors and inventors own their writing, work, and discoveries for a period of years so that other people can't use them without permission;

Vocabulary

DUTIES—taxes on things that are brought into the country or shipped out of it

IMPOSTS—taxes on imports (goods brought into the country)

EXCISES—taxes on things made, sold, or consumed within the country

NATURALIZATION—the process by which foreign-born people become citizens

To constitute **Tribunals** inferior to the supreme Court ⓭;

To define and punish **Piracies** and Felonies committed on the high Seas, and Offences against the Law of Nations ⓮;

To declare War, grant **Letters of Marque and Reprisal**, and make Rules concerning Captures on Land and Water ⓯;

To raise and support Armies, but no **Appropriation of Money** to that Use shall be for a longer Term than two Years ⓰;

To provide and maintain a Navy ⓱;

To make Rules for the Government and Regulation of the land and naval Forces ⓲;

To provide for calling forth the **Militia** to execute the Laws of the Union, suppress Insurrections and repel Invasions ⓳;

To provide for organizing, arming, and disciplining, the Militia, and for governing such Part of them as may be employed in the Service of the United States, reserving to the States respectively, the Appointment of the Officers, and the Authority of training the Militia according to the discipline prescribed by Congress ⓴;

ARTICLE I. ★ SECTION 8. (continued)

13. to create a federal court system that operates below the Supreme Court;

14. to describe and create penalties for piracy and crimes committed at sea and against international law;

15. to declare war, to authorize private ships to attack enemy ships, and to make rules about captured property on land or water;

16. to create and supply an army, but the money for it has to be reviewed every two years;

17. to create and supply a navy;

18. to make rules that control land and water forces;

19. to call the militia into service to make sure the laws of the federal government are followed, put down revolts within the country, or stop an invasion;

20. to organize, arm, and discipline the militia and to regulate it when it serves the whole country, letting the states choose their own officers and train their troops according to Congress's rules;

Vocabulary

TRIBUNAL—court

PIRACIES—attacks on and robberies of ships at sea

LETTERS OF MARQUE AND REPRISAL—permission to act as a pirate. Nations that didn't have a big navy sometimes let private ships attack enemy ships, essentially letting them be pirates in the service of their country.

APPROPRIATION OF MONEY—money set aside for a purpose

MILITIA—an army that's called together when there's a threat. The United States didn't have a standing army (one that's always in place) at the time the Constitution was written. People were expected to leave their jobs when there was a war and join the army, then go home when the fighting was over.

ORIGINAL TEXT

To exercise exclusive Legislation in all Cases whatsoever, over such District (not exceeding ten Miles square) as may, by Cession of particular States, and the Acceptance of Congress, become the Seat of the Government of the United States **21**, and to exercise like Authority over all Places purchased by the Consent of the Legislature of the State in which the Same shall be, for the Erection of Forts, Magazines, Arsenals, dock-Yards, and other needful Buildings **22**;—And

To make all Laws which shall be necessary and proper for carrying into Execution the foregoing Powers, and all other Powers vested by this Constitution in the Government of the United States, or in any Department or Officer thereof **23**.

21 to make all the laws for the district (which can't be bigger than ten miles square) that is given up by the states and accepted by Congress as the location of the federal government;

22 and to control all places that are located within a state but have been bought by the federal government, with the permission of the state legislature, for building forts, buildings for storing guns and ammunition, buildings for storing or making equipment for the military, docks for storing and repairing ships, and other buildings as are necessary;

23 and to make all laws that are needed and appropriate to carry out the powers listed above, and all other powers given by the Constitution to the federal government or any of its agencies or officials.

CONSTITUTION IN ACTION

POWERS OF CONGRESS

The Elastic Clause is the last line in Article I, Section 8, and it gives Congress the power to do everything that's "necessary and proper" to carry out its work or the work of the rest of government. It's called the Elastic Clause because it can stretch so far and gives Congress enormous authority. Many of the implied powers of Congress—the powers that aren't listed specifically—spring from the Elastic Clause.

For example, in 1819, the Supreme Court ruled unanimously in *McCulloch v. Maryland* that the Elastic Clause gave Congress the power to start a national bank. This is a power that isn't specifically listed in the Constitution.

ORIGINAL TEXT

SECTION 9.

The Migration or Importation of such Persons as any of the States now existing shall think proper to admit, shall not be prohibited by the Congress prior to the Year one thousand eight hundred and eight **1**, but a tax or duty may be imposed on such Importation, not exceeding ten dollars for each Person **2**.

1619
First enslaved Africans arrive in Jamestown, Virginia.

1808
The international slave trade in the United States ends, as allowed by the Constitution.

1861
War begins between the United States and the Confederate States of America over the issue of slavery.

1865
Civil War ends and slavery is abolished.

CONSTITUTION IN ACTION

WORDS USED AND NOT USED

The word "slavery" wasn't explicitly used in the Constitution until the 13th Amendment was ratified in 1865. The Framers talked about slavery earlier in the document—they just didn't use the word. Article I, Section 2, Clause 3 talks about how representatives were to be divided among the states, saying that "other persons" would be counted as three-fifths of a person. "Other persons" meant slaves. Article I, Section 9, Clause 1 talks about "migration or importation of such persons"—which meant the international slave trade.

The Constitution gave Congress enormous power. But it didn't allow an end to the international trade in human beings before 1808. Delegates from South

1. Bringing people into the country whom any of the existing states at the time the Constitution goes into effect want to bring in can't be stopped by Congress before 1808,

2. but a tax or duty of up to ten dollars can be collected for each person who is brought in.

> This refers to slaves.

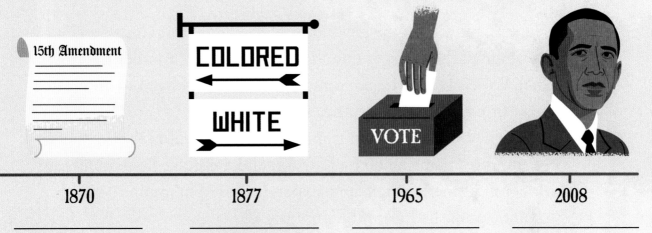

1870
15th Amendment gives Black men the right to vote.

1877
Reconstruction in the South ends, and segregation between Blacks and Whites increases.

1965
Voting Rights Act is passed, strengthening Black voting rights.

2008
Barack Obama is elected as the first African American president of the United States.

Carolina and Georgia insisted on a twenty-year cushion from the time the Constitution was ratified before the slave trade could be abolished. Congress did end the importation of slaves on January 1, 1808, the soonest it was able to do so, but in those twenty years, tens of thousands of people were brought to the United States in chains.

By that point, the international slave trade was no longer necessary to support the institution of slavery in the United States. Slave states in the Upper South, like Virginia, actually wanted the international slave trade banned so that they could sell their slaves to slaveholders in the Lower South for higher prices. The 1861 Confederate Constitution banned the international slave trade.

The privilege of the **Writ of Habeas Corpus** shall not be suspended, unless when in Cases of Rebellion or Invasion the public Safety may require it **3**.

No **Bill of Attainder** or **ex post facto Law** shall be passed **4**.

[No Capitation, or other direct, Tax shall be laid, unless in Proportion to the Census or enumeration herein before directed to be taken **5**.] *(Note: The section in brackets was clarified by the 16th Amendment* **6** *.)*

No Tax or Duty shall be laid on Articles exported from any State **7**.

No preference shall be given by any Regulation of Commerce or Revenue to the Ports of one State over those of another **8**: nor shall Vessels bound to, or from, one State, be obliged to enter, clear or pay Duties in another **9**.

No money shall be drawn from the Treasury, but in Consequence of Appropriations made by Law **10**; and a regular Statement and Account of the Receipts and Expenditures of all public Money shall be published from time to time **11**.

No Title of **Nobility** shall be granted by the United States **12**: And no Person holding any Office of Profit or Trust under them, shall, without the Consent of the Congress, accept of any present, Emolument, Office, or Title, of any kind whatever, from any King, Prince, or foreign State **13**.

ARTICLE I. ★ SECTION 9. (continued)

Vocabulary

WRIT OF HABEAS CORPUS—a requirement that the government explain to a judge or court why someone was arrested and release them if the explanation isn't good enough

BILL OF ATTAINDER—a law that declares someone guilty of a crime (instead of letting them have a trial where the government would have to prove they committed the crime)

3 The right of the writ of habeas corpus will not be taken away except in cases of rebellion or invasion when public safety is at risk.

4 No law will be passed that declares someone guilty of a crime, or that makes an action illegal and then tries people who already did it.

5 [No tax on the population or other direct tax will be put in place unless it's based on the size of the population as taken by the census.]

6 Note: Bracketed text changed by the 16th Amendment.* See page 140.

Changed to allow the federal government to tax income directly.

7 There will be no tax on exports.

8 Congressional rules on trade or taxes won't give better treatment to ports in some states over others.

9 Ships headed to or from one state don't have to pay import taxes in another state.

10 No money will be taken out of the treasury without being approved by law.

11 A regular statement of the money coming in and being spent will be published occasionally.

12 The federal government will not give a title of nobility to anyone,

13 and no one holding any federal office will accept any present, item of value, office, or title from a king, prince, or foreign country without permission from Congress.

CONSTITUTION IN ACTION

TITLES OF NOBILITY

Article I, Section 9 prohibits the federal government from granting titles. That's why you aren't Lady Olivia or Lord Jack. It's also why America has counties—the land held by a count—but no counts.

EX POST FACTO LAW—a law that makes something illegal and allows punishment of people who did it before the law made it illegal. Also a law that increases the punishment for a crime and applies the new punishment to people who committed the crime before the law was passed.

NOBILITY—aristocracy. "Duchess," "countess," and "earl" are examples of noble titles.

SECTION 10.

No State shall enter into any **Treaty**, **Alliance**, or **Confederation**; grant Letters of Marque and Reprisal; coin Money; emit Bills of Credit; make any Thing but gold and silver Coin a Tender in Payment of Debts; pass any Bill of Attainder, ex post facto Law, or Law impairing the Obligation of Contracts, or grant any Title of Nobility **1**.

No State shall, without the Consent of the Congress, lay any Imposts or Duties on Imports or Exports, except what may be absolutely necessary for executing it's inspection Laws **2**: and the net Produce of all Duties and Imposts, laid by any State on Imports or Exports, shall be for the Use of the Treasury of the United States **3**; and all such Laws shall be subject to the Revision and Control of the Congress **4**.

No State shall, without the Consent of Congress, lay any Duty of Tonnage, keep Troops, or Ships of War in time of Peace **5**, enter into any Agreement or Compact with another State, or with a foreign Power **6**, or engage in War, unless actually invaded, or in such imminent Danger as will not admit of delay **7**.

DID YOU KNOW?

Article I, Section 10 lists powers the states gave up upon joining the Union. This was part of the effort to make the federal government stronger and to identify the jobs of the federal government—like creating an army and manufacturing money.

Vocabulary

TREATY—an official agreement between countries

ALLIANCE—an agreement to work together or be on the same side

CONFEDERATION—a loose organization in which the lower level (like states) has more power than the higher level (like the federal government)

1. No state will make its own treaties, make agreements with other countries, or join international organizations; authorize private ships to attack enemy ships; manufacture money; issue its own credit; allow payment of debts by anything other than gold or silver coin; or pass a law that declares someone guilty of a crime or one that makes an action illegal and then tries people who did it before it was illegal, pass a law interfering with contracts, or grant titles of nobility.

2. No state, without permission from Congress, will tax any goods coming in or going out, except when it's necessary for carrying out its laws for inspecting goods,

3. and money raised by state taxes on imports and exports goes to the federal government,

4. and all laws about state import and export taxes can be changed by and are under the control of Congress.

5. No state, without permission from Congress, will charge any ship for entering, leaving, or staying in port; keep an army or warships during peacetime;

6. make any agreements with other states or countries;

7. or make war, unless they're invaded or they're in such danger that there isn't time to tell Congress before they have to act.

Article II.

Article II sets up the executive branch, which includes the president, vice president, and executive agencies like the State Department and the Justice Department. It explains how the president and vice president will be elected, the powers and responsibilities of the president, and how to remove him or her from office.

SECTION 1.

The executive Power shall be vested in a President of the United States of America ❶. **He** shall hold his Office during the Term of four Years, and, together with the Vice President, chosen for the same Term, be elected, as follows ❷:

Each State shall appoint, in such Manner as the Legislature thereof may direct, a Number of Electors, equal to the whole Number of Senators and Representatives to which the State may be entitled in the Congress ❸: but no Senator or Representative, or Person holding an Office of Trust or Profit under the United States, shall be appointed an Elector ❹.

[The Electors shall meet in their respective States, and vote by Ballot for two Persons, of whom one at least shall not be an Inhabitant of the same State with themselves ❺. And they shall make a List of all the Persons voted for, and of the Number of Votes for each; which List they shall sign and certify, and transmit sealed to the Seat of the Government of the United States, directed to the President of the Senate ❻.

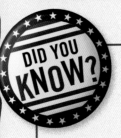

DID YOU KNOW?

Article II, Section 1 sets up the Electoral College. In this case, "college" means a group. Individual voters don't vote for the president and vice president. They vote for electors, or voters, who actually choose the president and vice president. The Framers put an extra layer between the people and the president out of fear that people might elect someone unqualified. They hoped that the electors would make sure the choice was a wise one.

If electors don't vote the way they said they would, they're called "faithless electors." There have been more than 150 faithless electors in US history, but they've never changed who became president.

TRANSLATION

1. The power to put federal laws and policies into practice will belong to a president of the country.

2. He will be in office for four years and, with a vice president who serves the same amount of time, will be chosen as follows:

3. Each state, according to its own laws, will choose a number of voters in the Electoral College that is the same as the number of senators and representatives that state holds in Congress,

4. but no senator, representative, or anyone with a job in the federal government will be chosen as an elector.

5. [The electors will meet in their own states and vote by ballot for two people, and at least one of them has to be from a different state than the elector.

6. The electors will make a list of all the people who got votes and how many votes they each got, and they will sign, confirm, and seal the list before sending it to the president of the Senate—that is, the vice president of the United States—in Washington, DC.

CONSTITUTION IN ACTION

EXECUTIVE PRIVILEGE

Executive privilege is a president's ability to keep things they say or do private. Refusing Congress, the courts, and the public access to some materials allows the president and his or her advisors to talk about issues freely. Executive privilege isn't mentioned in the Constitution and is therefore controversial. People who believe a president should be able to withhold information point to the president's responsibility to see that laws are faithfully executed.

Vocabulary

HE—The masculine pronoun is used in the Constitution, but the articles apply the same to a female president, lawmaker, or judge.

ORIGINAL TEXT

The President of the Senate shall, in the Presence of the Senate and House of Representatives, open all the Certificates, and the Votes shall then be counted. The Person having the greatest Number of Votes shall be the President, if such Number be a Majority of the whole Number of Electors appointed **7**; and if there be more than one who have such Majority, and have an equal Number of Votes, then the House of Representatives shall immediately chuse by Ballot one of them for President **8**; and if no Person have a Majority, then from the five highest on the List the said House shall in like Manner chuse the President **9**. But in chusing the President, the Votes shall be taken by States, the Representation from each State having one Vote; A quorum for this Purpose shall consist of a Member or Members from two thirds of the States, and a Majority of all the States shall be necessary to a Choice **10**. In every Case, after the Choice of the President, the Person having the greatest Number of Votes of the Electors shall be the Vice President. But if there should remain two or more who have equal Votes, the Senate shall chuse from them by Ballot the Vice President **11**.] *(Note: This clause in brackets was superseded by the 12th Amendment **12**.)*

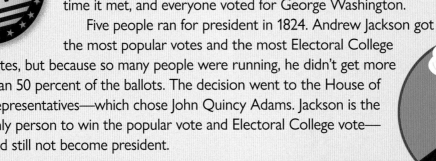

DID YOU KNOW?

The only unanimous vote in the Electoral College was in 1789, the first time it met, and everyone voted for George Washington.

Five people ran for president in 1824. Andrew Jackson got the most popular votes and the most Electoral College votes, but because so many people were running, he didn't get more than 50 percent of the ballots. The decision went to the House of Representatives—which chose John Quincy Adams. Jackson is the only person to win the popular vote and Electoral College vote—and still not become president.

7 The vice president will, in front of both houses of Congress, open the lists and count the votes. The person who gets the most votes will be president, as long as a majority of all the electors voted for that person.

8 If more than one person has a majority of votes by electors and they're tied, then the House of Representatives will take a ballot vote to choose one of them to be president.

9 If no one gets a majority of all the votes, then the House of Representatives will take a ballot vote to choose one of the five highest candidates on the list to be president.

10 In choosing the president, the vote is taken by states, and each state has one vote; a quorum will be made up of at least one member from two-thirds of the states, and the winner has to get a majority of all states.

11 In all cases, after the president has been chosen, whoever got the next highest number of votes becomes vice president. If there's a tie, the Senate will take a ballot vote to choose one of them to be vice president.]

12 Note: Bracketed text changed by the 12th Amendment.*
See page 126.

*Changed so that electors make clear which person they're voting for to be president and which to be vice president. And if the House of Representatives is supposed to choose the president but hasn't by the day the president is supposed to take office, then the vice president acts as president.

PRESIDENT

VICE PRESIDENT

ORIGINAL TEXT

The Congress may determine the Time of chusing the Electors, and the Day on which they shall give their Votes; which Day shall be the same throughout the United States **13**.

No Person except a natural born Citizen, or a Citizen of the United States, at the time of the Adoption of this Constitution, shall be eligible to the Office of President **14**; neither shall any Person be eligible to that Office who shall not have attained to the Age of thirty five Years, and been fourteen Years a Resident within the United States **15**.

CONSTITUTION IN ACTION

PRESIDENTIAL SUCCESSION

Article II, Section 1 says that if the president dies, resigns, or is unable to do the job, the vice president takes over. The 25th Amendment clarifies that language, saying that when a vice president takes over, the vice president doesn't just *act* as president but actually *becomes* the president.

The Constitution gives Congress the power to choose who comes next after the vice president. The Presidential Succession Act of 1947 is the law by which Congress chose the order, which is: the Speaker of the House, the president pro tempore of the Senate, and then the Cabinet officers in the order in which the departments were created. The secretaries of state, treasury, and defense and the attorney general were the original Cabinet secretaries.

After them come the secretaries of the interior, agriculture, commerce, labor, health and human services, housing and urban development, transportation, energy, education, veterans affairs, and homeland security.

If a person is not constitutionally eligible to be president (if he or she isn't old enough or wasn't a citizen from birth), that person would be skipped and the job would go to the next person.

13. Congress can decide when electors are chosen and on which day they vote; that day will be the same for all states in the country.

14. No one except a citizen of the United States from birth, or a citizen of the United States at the time this Constitution goes into effect, can be elected president;

15. and no person can be elected president unless they're at least thirty-five years old and have been a resident of the country for at least fourteen years.

ORIGINAL TEXT

[In Case of the Removal of the President from Office, or of his Death, Resignation, or Inability to discharge the Powers and Duties of the said Office, the Same shall devolve on the Vice President ⑯, and the Congress may by Law provide for the Case of Removal, Death, Resignation or Inability, both of the President and Vice President, declaring what Officer shall then act as President, and such Officer shall act accordingly, until the Disability be removed, or a President shall be elected ⑰.] *(Note: This clause in brackets was modified by the 20th and 25th Amendments ⑱.)* The President shall, at stated Times, receive for his Services, a Compensation, which shall neither be encreased nor diminished during the Period for which he shall have been elected ⑲, and he shall not receive within that Period any other Emolument from the United States, or any of them ⑳.

Before he enter on the Execution of his Office, he shall take the following Oath or Affirmation: "I do solemnly swear (or affirm) that I will faithfully **execute** the Office of President of the United States, and will to the best of my Ability, preserve, protect and defend the Constitution of the United States" ㉑.

CONSTITUTION IN ACTION

OATHS

An oath is a serious promise. The Framers thought the president's oath to defend the Constitution was important enough to write it into the Constitution itself. Both state and federal employees also swear to support and defend the Constitution. Officers of all branches of the armed forces also take an oath, and so do immigrants when they become citizens.

George Washington was the first person to take the president's oath. He placed his hand on a Bible as he spoke, which began a tradition but isn't required. He also added the words "so help me God." They aren't required, either.

Vocabulary

EXECUTE—to carry something out or perform a task; to do the job

TRANSLATION

(16) [If the president is removed from office, dies, steps down, or is unable to do the job, the authority and responsibility of the office will be given to the vice president.

(17) Congress can make laws about what will happen if both the president and vice president are removed from office, die, step down, or are unable to do their job and can declare which official will act as the president, and that official will hold the office until the president or vice president is able to work again or a president is elected.]

(18) Note: Bracketed text changed by the 20th★ and 25th† Amendments. See pages 150 and 162.

★Changed so that if the president-elect dies before taking office, the vice president–elect becomes president. If a president isn't chosen or hasn't qualified before they're supposed to take the oath of office, the vice president–elect acts as president until the president is in place.

†Changed so that if a president dies, leaves, or is removed from office, the vice president becomes president (not acting president).

(19) The president will be paid at specific times, and the amount he is paid can't increase or decrease during his time in office,

(20) and while in office, the president will not receive anything else of value from the federal government or from any state.

(21) Before taking office, the president will take the following oath or affirmation:

"I do solemnly swear (or affirm) that I will faithfully execute the office of president of the United States and will to the best of my ability preserve, protect, and defend the Constitution of the United States."

ORIGINAL TEXT

SECTION 2.

The President shall be **Commander in Chief** of the Army and Navy of the United States, and of the Militia of the several States, when called into the actual Service of the United States **1**; he may require the Opinion, in writing, of the principal Officer in each of the **executive Departments**, upon any Subject relating to the Duties of their respective Offices **2**, and he shall have Power to grant **Reprieves** and **Pardons** for Offences against the United States, except in Cases of Impeachment **3**.

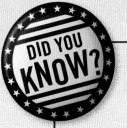

DID YOU KNOW?

The Constitution gives the president the power to pardon people convicted of crimes, setting aside their punishment. The conviction still stays on their record, however. Pardons can be given only for federal crimes. A president can't issue a pardon to allow someone who was impeached and convicted to keep their government job. Presidents can pardon people before they're prosecuted, but they can't pardon crimes that haven't happened yet.

Vocabulary

COMMANDER IN CHIEF—the person in charge of the country's military forces

EXECUTIVE DEPARTMENTS—agencies in the executive branch, such as the Department of the Treasury, Department of Agriculture, and Department of State. Heads of the executive departments are in the Cabinet, which advises the president.

REPRIEVE—putting off the punishment for a crime

PARDON—a cancellation of the punishment for a crime; forgiving the crime

TRANSLATION

1. The president will occasionally give Congress updates on the state of the country
2. and suggest laws that are necessary and useful;
3. the president may, in unusual situations, call one or both chambers of Congress into session,
4. and if they can't agree on when to end their sessions, the president can dismiss them until a time he chooses.
5. The president will meet with ambassadors and other officials;
6. he will make sure that the laws are carried out
7. and will pick all officers of the federal government.

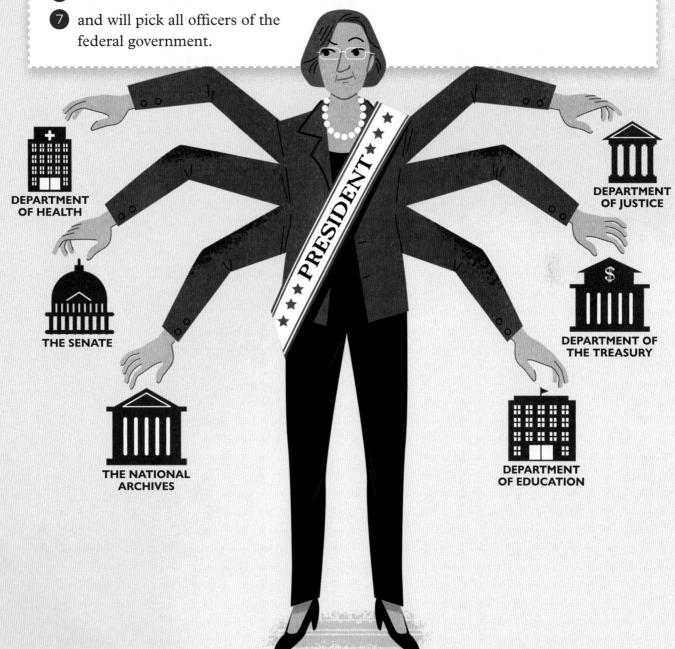

DEPARTMENT OF HEALTH

THE SENATE

THE NATIONAL ARCHIVES

DEPARTMENT OF JUSTICE

DEPARTMENT OF THE TREASURY

DEPARTMENT OF EDUCATION

PRESIDENT

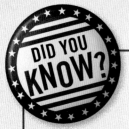

DID YOU KNOW?

Article II, Section 3 says that the president should give a State of the Union address to Congress. George Washington gave the first address on January 8, 1790, when he spoke to Congress about foreign policy, defense, immigration, and other important topics.

Thomas Jefferson, our nation's third president, thought that speaking to Congress was too much like a speech by the English king, so he sent his message to Congress in writing. That may not have been his only reason, though—Jefferson was a terrible public speaker but a very good writer. (He wrote the Declaration of Independence.) For the next century, presidents sent their State of the Union messages as letters. In 1913, Woodrow Wilson delivered his State of the Union address to Congress in person, and every president since has followed his example.

In the nineteenth century, presidents included specific information on the economy and the national budget in their State of the Union addresses. Today, that information is delivered in separate documents and any talk about the economy is more general.

Because of technological changes, such as television and the internet, presidents are now talking not only to Congress, but to the American people, and they use the chance to try and build support for their programs and goals. In 1947, Harry Truman became the first president to deliver a televised State of the Union address.

CONSTITUTION IN ACTION

EXECUTIVE ORDERS

Part of being familiar with the Constitution is knowing what *isn't* in it. The Constitution doesn't directly give presidents the authority to issue executive orders. But sometimes they do it anyway. The ability to issue such orders is implied by Article II: The president "shall take Care that the Laws be faithfully executed." Only Congress can make federal laws, so the president can't issue an order that creates a law. The president also can't tell private citizens or members of the other branches of government what to do. And because all bills dealing with spending have to start in the House of Representatives, the president can't issue orders that take money from the Treasury.

SECTION 4.

The President, Vice President and all civil Officers of the United States, shall be removed from Office on Impeachment for, and Conviction of, Treason, **Bribery**, or other **high Crimes and Misdemeanors** ❶.

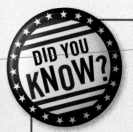

Only three presidents—Andrew Johnson, Bill Clinton, and Donald Trump—have been impeached, but none of them were found guilty and removed from office. Another president—Richard Nixon—was facing impeachment but resigned from office before Congress had a chance to begin the proceedings.

Andrew Johnson, Abraham Lincoln's vice president, became president when Lincoln was assassinated. Many people in Congress didn't trust him because he was a Southerner and seemed too sympathetic to the just-defeated Confederacy. Congress passed a law saying that the president couldn't fire his Cabinet officials without the Senate's permission. When Johnson fired his secretary of war, the House wrote eleven articles of impeachment against him. Most of them were about firing the secretary of war, but one said that he gave speeches "with a loud voice." Johnson was found not guilty by one vote.

In 1998, Bill Clinton was charged with giving false testimony to a grand jury about his relationship with a young woman and obstructing justice in an effort to stop an investigation. The Senate found Clinton not guilty on both charges.

Donald Trump was impeached on charges of abuse of power and obstruction of Congress in December 2019. He was found not guilty in February 2020.

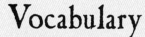

Vocabulary

BRIBERY—the act of offering or taking money or a favor in return for something

HIGH CRIMES AND MISDEMEANORS—This term can be understood in different ways. Serious crimes probably count, but the Framers were focused on misuse of government power.

1 The president, vice president, and all federal officers will be removed from office if they are impeached and found guilty of treason, bribery, or other high crimes and misdemeanors.

CONSTITUTION IN ACTION

HIGH CRIMES AND MISDEMEANORS

Article II, Section 4 says that civil officers of the United States, such as the president, can be removed from office for committing "high Crimes and Misdemeanors." Like the impeachment process, which starts in the House of Representatives and then moves to the Senate, the "high Crimes and Misdemeanors" standard was taken from England. While the phrase has never been precisely defined, the Framers of the Constitution could look to hundreds of years of British practice using it. Studying this practice suggests that "high" refers to both crimes and misdemeanors ("high crimes" and "high misdemeanors"). It doesn't mean "serious" but instead something like "related to public office"—the sort of bad behavior that only a public official could engage in. That means that ordinary crimes might not qualify, and also that people can be impeached for things that aren't crimes. (Most impeachments, in England before the Revolution and in America after the Constitution, did not identify a crime that the person had committed.) As Alexander Hamilton explained it, impeachable offenses come "from the misconduct of public men, or in other words from the abuse or violation of some public trust."

What counts as an impeachable abuse of power isn't totally clear, but there are three clear examples that have been used as grounds for impeachment in the past. They all come from violations of the principle that the government is supposed to serve the people. Government officials are supposed to use their power to benefit the public interest rather than themselves.

First, officials might use their power to make themselves richer. That is corruption. In some ways, it's also covered by the reference to bribery and the emoluments clauses. Second, officials might use their power to interfere with democracy, so that they could keep their jobs even if they didn't deserve to. That is corruption of the democratic process. Third, officials might use their power to punish people they don't like, even if those people haven't done anything wrong. That is tyranny. All of these involve betrayals of the public trust.

It is also clear that people are not supposed to be impeached just for doing a bad job. A suggested alternative to "high Crimes and Misdemeanors" was "maladministration," which sounds more like doing a bad job. The Framers thought that term was too vague and too broad, so they rejected that suggestion and wrote "high Crimes and Misdemeanors."

Q: **WHAT ARE HIGH CRIMES AND MISDEMEANORS?**

A: _____

FRAUD

INTIMIDATION

TREASON

MISUSE OF PUBLIC FUNDS

PERJURY

LYING

BRIBERY

OBSTRUCTION OF JUSTICE

CONSTITUTION IN ACTION

IMPEACHMENT

Impeachment charges are brought by the House of Representatives and a trial is held in the Senate. If the person being tried is someone other than the president, the vice president, as president of the Senate, runs the trial. But if the president is on trial, the chief justice of the Supreme Court is in charge. Being impeached means being accused; it's possible to be impeached and found not guilty.

If a president (or other official) is found guilty in an impeachment trial, they're removed from office and usually can't hold any federal office. The Supreme Court has ruled that impeachment can't be appealed to the courts. If a president is found guilty, the verdict is final and he or she must leave office.

Article III.

Article III sets up the judicial system, or courts. It describes what kinds of cases can be heard, gives details on how trials will be run, and defines treason. The Constitution is much less detailed about the judicial branch than it is about the legislative and executive branches. For example, the Constitution doesn't say how many Supreme Court justices there should be.

ORIGINAL TEXT

SECTION 1.

The judicial Power of the United States, shall be vested in one supreme Court ❶, and in such inferior Courts as the Congress may from time to time ordain and establish ❷. The Judges, both of the supreme and inferior Courts, shall hold their Offices during good Behaviour ❸, and shall, at stated Times, receive for their Services, a Compensation, which shall not be diminished during their Continuance in Office ❹.

CONSTITUTION IN ACTION

COURT SYSTEM

The United States has a dual court system, meaning it has both federal and state courts. Most cases are heard in state courts. Each state has the power to set up its court system the way it wants, and those systems vary.

The Constitution set up the United States Supreme Court, which is the top court in the country. It also allowed Congress to set up lower courts. When people lose a case in a lower court, they can appeal it, or ask for it to be retried, at a higher level. That process can take a case all the way up to the United States Supreme Court.

The Supreme Court decides which cases it will hear. It doesn't have to hear all the cases people appeal to it and actually accepts very few. If the Supreme Court refuses to hear a case, the decision of the lower court stands. But if the Supreme Court does rule on a case, its decision is final.

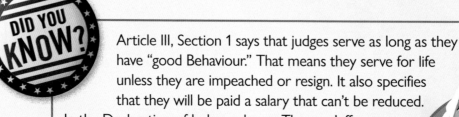

DID YOU KNOW?

Article III, Section 1 says that judges serve as long as they have "good Behaviour." That means they serve for life unless they are impeached or resign. It also specifies that they will be paid a salary that can't be reduced. In the Declaration of Independence, Thomas Jefferson complained that the English king George III had made judges dependent on him for their ability to stay in office and for how much they would get paid. That could affect the judges' independence.

TRANSLATION

1. The judicial authority of the United States will be placed in one Supreme Court

2. and in lower federal courts that Congress can make as needed.

3. The judges in all courts will hold their offices as long as their behavior is acceptable

4. and will at specific times be paid for their work, and their pay can't be decreased while they're in office.

US Supreme Court

12 Regional US Courts of Appeals

94 US District Courts

SECTION 2.

The judicial Power shall extend to all Cases, in **Law and Equity**, arising under this Constitution, the Laws of the United States, and Treaties made, or which shall be made, under their Authority ❶; to all Cases affecting Ambassadors, other public Ministers and Consuls ❷; to all Cases of admiralty and maritime Jurisdiction ❸; to Controversies to which the United States shall be a Party ❹; to Controversies between two or more States; [between a State and Citizens of another State;] between Citizens of different States ❺, between Citizens of the same State claiming Lands under Grants of different States ❻, and between a State, or the Citizens thereof, and foreign States, Citizens or Subjects ❼. *(Note: This section in brackets is modified by the 11th Amendment ❽.)*

DID YOU KNOW?

One of the powers that allows government branches to check one another is "judicial review." That's the Supreme Court's power to rule that the laws Congress passes, or things the president does, are unconstitutional. Article III, Section 2 doesn't mention judicial review. The Court first used this power to rule an act of Congress unconstitutional in 1803. Many people see judicial review as a key part of the checks and balances of our government, while others worry that unelected judges can overturn acts of elected officials.

Vocabulary

LAW AND EQUITY—law and justice

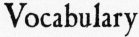

1. Federal judges can decide only certain kinds of cases, including cases involving the Constitution, the laws of the federal government, or agreements with foreign countries;

2. all cases involving ambassadors, other public ministers, and consuls;

3. all cases regarding things that happen at sea;

4. cases involving the federal government;

5. disagreements between two or more states, [or between a state and citizens of another state,] or between citizens of different states;

6. between citizens of the same state if different states give them the same piece of land;

7. and between a state, or citizens of a state, and foreign countries (or their citizens or subjects).

8. Note: Bracketed text changed by the 11th Amendment in federal court.* See page 125.

   Changed so that citizens of one state can't sue another state.

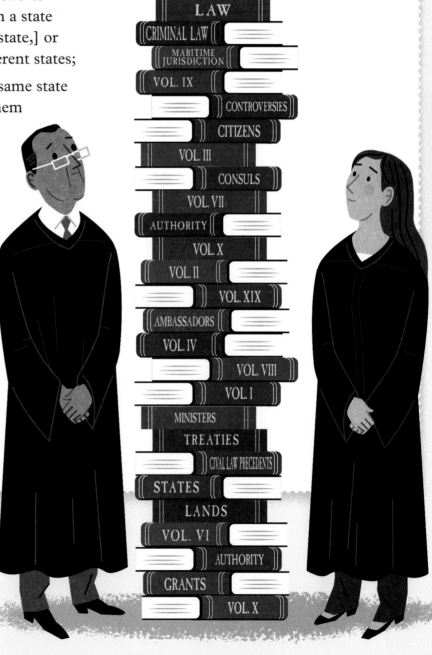

ORIGINAL TEXT

In all Cases affecting Ambassadors, other public Ministers and Consuls, and those in which a State shall be Party, the supreme Court shall have **original Jurisdiction** 9. In all the other Cases before mentioned, the supreme Court shall have **appellate Jurisdiction**, both as to Law and Fact, with such Exceptions, and under such Regulations as the Congress shall make 10. The Trial of all Crimes, except in Cases of Impeachment, shall be by **Jury** 11; and such Trial shall be held in the State where the said Crimes shall have been committed 12; but when not committed within any State, the Trial shall be at such Place or Places as the Congress may by Law have directed 13.

TRANSLATION

⑨ In all cases dealing with ambassadors, other public ministers, and consuls, and in cases in which a state is on one side, the case starts in the Supreme Court.

⑩ All other cases listed previously can be appealed to the Supreme Court after some other court decides, and the Supreme Court can look at both the law and the facts of a case, though with any exceptions Congress makes, and according to its rules.

⑪ All trials except impeachments are by jury,

⑫ and trials will be held in the state in which the crime was committed,

⑬ but if the crime wasn't committed in any state, Congress decides where the trial will be.

CONSTITUTION IN ACTION

JURIES

Article III says there must be a jury trial in all cases except impeachments and that the trial will be held where the crime was committed.

Juries are groups of regular people—not judges—who listen to evidence in a court case and decide if the person on trial is guilty or not guilty. Juries provide extra protection for citizens because the government can't pressure them in the way it might pressure a judge who gets his or her job from, and is paid by, the state. The first jury in the colonies met in 1630 to judge a murder trial in Plymouth Colony (Massachusetts).

Vocabulary

ORIGINAL JURISDICTION—the authority of the Supreme Court to hear some cases directly, without those cases starting in a lower court. The Supreme Court has "original jurisdiction" in those cases.

APPELLATE JURISDICTION—Most cases that reach the Supreme Court were heard first in a lower

court and then appealed. The Supreme Court has "appellate jurisdiction" in cases that have to start in a lower court.

JURY—a group of people who listen to evidence in a court case and decide if the person who's been charged is guilty or not guilty

ORIGINAL TEXT

SECTION 3.

Treason against the United States, shall consist only in levying War against them, or in adhering to their Enemies, giving them Aid and Comfort ❶. No Person shall be convicted of Treason unless on the Testimony of two Witnesses to the same overt Act, or on Confession in open Court ❷.

The Congress shall have Power to declare the Punishment of Treason ❸, but no **Attainder of Treason** shall work **Corruption of Blood**, or **Forfeiture** except during the Life of the Person attainted ❹.

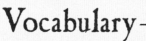
DID YOU KNOW?

The Constitution defines only one crime—treason—and it defines it very narrowly. In England, charges of treason were sometimes used to keep people from criticizing the government. The Framers didn't want that to happen in the United States so they made it very hard to prove a treason charge. Supreme Court rulings have made it even harder to convict someone of treason. A person who is suspected of treason is more likely to be charged with spying or a similar crime.

Vocabulary

ATTAINDER OF TREASON—having to give up rights and property after being convicted of treason

CORRUPTION OF BLOOD—not letting a person pass property down to his or her children as part of the punishment for a crime

FORFEITURE—giving something up, like money or property, as a punishment

TRANSLATION

1. Treason is defined as waging war against the United States or helping its enemies.

2. No one will be found guilty of treason unless two people say in court that the person did it or the person confesses in court.

3. Congress decides the punishment for treason,

4. but a treason conviction can't keep the convicted person's relatives from inheriting their rightful property after the person's death.

CONSTITUTION IN ACTION

CORRUPTION OF BLOOD

Article III, Section 3 says that "no Attainder of Treason shall work Corruption of Blood." Corruption of blood is an old concept that means the heirs of a convicted person aren't allowed to have their inheritance as punishment. This was a big deal to people whose wealth depended on inheriting an estate. The Constitution outlaws corruption of blood, saying that punishment stops with the person who committed the crime—their children or other heirs aren't affected.

Article IV.

Article IV talks about the relationships of the states to one another and between the states and federal government.

ORIGINAL TEXT

SECTION 1.

Full Faith and Credit shall be given in each State to the public Acts, Records, and judicial Proceedings of every other State **1**. And the Congress may by general Laws prescribe the Manner in which such Acts, Records and Proceedings shall be proved, and the Effect thereof **2**.

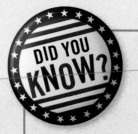

The Full Faith and Credit Clause requires states to recognize other states' records, like birth certificates and court verdicts. Under the Articles of Confederation, the states treated one another like independent countries, but the Constitution tried to unify the country and Article IV was an important part of this.

1 Each state will recognize the laws, records, and court verdicts of every other state.

2 Congress can decide how these acts, records, and verdicts can be proved in other states' courts and what effect they will have.

SECTION 2.

The Citizens of each State shall be entitled to all Privileges and Immunities of Citizens in the several States **1**.

A Person charged in any State with Treason, Felony, or other Crime, who shall flee from Justice, and be found in another State **2**, shall on Demand of the executive Authority of the State from which he fled, be delivered up **3**, to be removed to the State having Jurisdiction of the Crime **4**.

[No Person held to Service or Labour in one State, under the Laws thereof, escaping into another, shall, in Consequence of any Law or Regulation therein, be discharged from such Service or Labour, but shall be delivered up on Claim of the Party to whom such Service or Labour may be due **5**.] *(Note: This clause in brackets is superseded by the 13th Amendment **6**.)*

DID YOU KNOW?

Dred Scott was a slave whose master took him into free territory. Then the master moved with Scott and Scott's family back to a slave state. Scott sued for his freedom in federal court in Missouri, arguing that his residence in a free territory had made him free. He died in 1858, the year after the Supreme Court decided that he wasn't a citizen and didn't have the right to sue. Dred Scott didn't live to see Abraham Lincoln elected president, the Civil War fought, or the slaves freed—but he helped make all those things happen.

NORTHERN STATES

DRED SCOTT

① Citizens of one state who visit other states get the same rights as the people who live there.

② A person charged by a state with treason or another crime, who runs away from law enforcement in that state and is found in another state,

③ will, at the request of the governor of the state from which he or she fled,

④ be returned to the state in which the crime was committed.

⑤ [No slave who escapes to another state will, based on the laws of the state to which he or she fled, be freed, but will be returned based on the claim of the slave owner.]

⑥ Note: Bracketed text changed by the 13th Amendment.* See page 130.

Changed to end slavery and forced labor, except as a punishment for crime.

CONSTITUTION IN ACTION

DRED SCOTT V. SANDFORD, 1857

In *Dred Scott v. Sandford*, 1857, the Supreme Court said that no Black person, slave or free, could be a United States citizen. That meant Dred Scott didn't have the right to sue in federal court. The Court didn't have to say anything else in the case. But it went on to say that the Missouri Compromise of 1820, which banned slavery in some federal territories, was unconstitutional. In *Dred Scott*, the Court ruled that Congress could not outlaw slavery anywhere. Northerners were afraid that if Congress didn't have the right to keep slavery out of some areas, the whole nation would become slave territory. The *Dred Scott* decision upset a lot of people, helped make slavery the main issue in the 1860 election, and was a cause of the Civil War.

Most people consider *Dred Scott v. Sandford* to be the worst decision the Supreme Court ever made. In fact, it was so bad that the Court even made a typo in the case title: Scott's owner's name was Sanford.

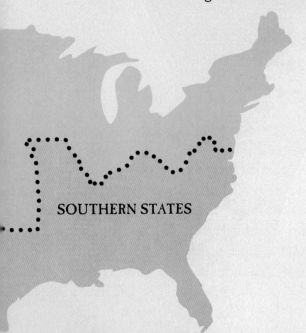

SOUTHERN STATES

ORIGINAL TEXT

SECTION 3.

New States may be admitted by the Congress into this Union; but no new State shall be formed or erected within the Jurisdiction of any other State ❶; nor any State be formed by the Junction of two or more States, or Parts of States, without the Consent of the Legislatures of the States concerned as well as of the Congress ❷.

The Congress shall have Power to dispose of and make all needful Rules and Regulations respecting the Territory or other Property belonging to the United States ❸; and nothing in this Constitution shall be so construed as to Prejudice any Claims of the United States, or of any particular State ❹.

CONSTITUTION IN ACTION

CREATING NEW STATES

West Virginia was created out of Virginia in 1863. When Virginia seceded, Virginia's western counties didn't want to leave the Union. They declared that they were the true government of Virginia and Lincoln agreed. Then they consented to the formation of a new state (themselves!) and Lincoln and Congress approved. That would seem to be unconstitutional under Article IV, but the clause prohibiting the creation of new states out of existing ones seems to just require the state's consent. That's true for the clause about creating new states by combining others, as well. (Kentucky was created out of Virginia in 1792, and Maine was part of Massachusetts until it became a separate state in 1820.)

TRANSLATION

1. New states can be added to the country by Congress, but no new state will be created inside another state,

2. and no state will be formed by combining two or more states or parts of states without permission from the governments of the states involved and from Congress.

3. Congress has the authority to make necessary rules and laws for all land and property belonging to the federal government,

4. and nothing in this Constitution will be interpreted so that it hurts the claims of the federal government or any state.

CONSTITUTION IN ACTION

TERRITORIES

The United States has five inhabited territories: Puerto Rico and the US Virgin Islands, both of which are in the Caribbean, and Guam, American Samoa, and the Northern Mariana Islands in the Pacific.

Not all constitutional rights apply to people in the territories. In 1776, Americans revolted because they were taxed but didn't have representation in England's Parliament. Yet today, the US territories pay taxes, but each territory has only one non-voting member in the House of Representatives. Their people serve in the army and can be drafted, but they can't vote for president. And veterans who live in the territories do not get as much help as those who live in a state.

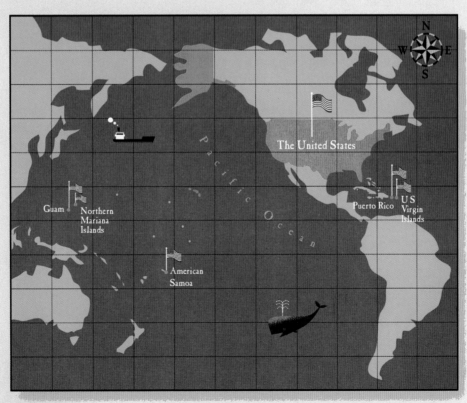

SECTION 4.

The United States shall guarantee to every State in this Union a **Republican Form of Government**, and shall protect each of them against Invasion ❶; and on Application of the Legislature, or of the Executive (when the Legislature cannot be convened), against domestic Violence ❷.

DID YOU KNOW?

When some states seceded from, or left, the Union in 1860 and 1861, they formed the Confederate States of America. They elected Jefferson Davis to be their president, and they wrote their own constitution that protected slavery. The United States refused to recognize the legality of secession. Abraham Lincoln argued that the Confederate states had never left the Union; they had just been taken over by rebels. Instead of having Congress declare war on the Confederacy, he pointed to the Guarantee Clause of Article IV, Section 4 and the Faithful Execution Clause of Article II, Section 3 as justification for fighting the Confederates.

Vocabulary

REPUBLICAN FORM OF GOVERNMENT—a government in which ultimate power is held by the people and their elected representatives. A republic has an elected head rather than a hereditary king or queen.

TRANSLATION

1. The federal government will guarantee that every state in the country has a democratic form of government and will protect each of them from invasion,

2. and when a state legislature, or governor (if the legislature isn't meeting), asks, the federal government will protect each state from major uprisings within the state.

STATES THAT SECEDED FROM THE UNITED STATES TO FORM THE CONFEDERATE STATES OF AMERICA

Abraham Lincoln was elected president in 1860 and took office on March 4, 1861. But before he took the oath, seven states seceded from the United States; four others followed.

South Carolina: December 20, 1860

Mississippi: January 9, 1861

Florida: January 10, 1861

Alabama: January 11, 1861

Georgia: January 19, 1861

Louisiana: January 26, 1861

Texas: February 1, 1861

Virginia: April 17, 1861

Arkansas: May 6, 1861

North Carolina: May 20, 1861

Tennessee: June 8, 1861

Article V.

Article V explains how the Constitution can be amended, or changed.

The Congress, whenever two thirds of both Houses shall deem it necessary, shall propose Amendments to this Constitution ❶, or, on the Application of the Legislatures of two thirds of the several States, shall call a Convention for proposing Amendments ❷, which, in either Case, shall be valid to all Intents and Purposes, as Part of this Constitution, when ratified by the Legislatures of three fourths of the several States, or by Conventions in three fourths thereof, as the one or the other Mode of Ratification may be proposed by the Congress ❸; Provided that no Amendment which may be made prior to the Year One thousand eight hundred and eight shall in any Manner affect the first and fourth Clauses in the Ninth Section of the first Article ❹; and that no State, without its Consent, shall be deprived of its equal **Suffrage** in the Senate ❺.

CONSTITUTION IN ACTION

AN AMENDMENT VERSUS A LAW

Constitutional amendments are much harder to put in place—and much harder to take out—than a regular law, so Congress deals with most issues by passing laws. An amendment can be reversed by another amendment (and this has happened only once—the 21st Amendment overturned the 18th, ending a constitutional ban on alcohol). But most of the time, amendments are saved for major changes that are meant to be permanent, like ending slavery or giving women the right to vote.

More than ten thousand amendments have been proposed since the Constitution was written, but only twenty-seven of them have made it into the document. A few of the amendments that were proposed but never ratified were proposals to abolish the Senate (1876), have a three-president council (1878), rename the country "the United States of Earth" (1893), have a national vote before entering a war where everyone who votes for the war has to volunteer for the army (1916, after World War I started but before the United States entered), and guarantee the right to a pollution-free environment (1971).

Vocabulary

SUFFRAGE—the right to vote

ARTICLE V.

1 When two-thirds of both the House of Representatives and the Senate decide it's necessary, Congress can propose additions to the Constitution,

2 or two-thirds of the state legislatures can call for a meeting to suggest changes,

3 and either way, those additions or changes become an official part of the Constitution once they're accepted by three-fourths of the state legislatures or by meetings in three-fourths of the states, depending on which way Congress suggests to do it.

4 But no amendment ending the international slave trade can be passed before 1808, interfering with Article I, Section 9, Clause 1 or Article I, Section 9, Clause 4 (see page 42),

5 and no state, without its permission, will lose its equal representation in the Senate.

DID YOU KNOW?

The Framers knew that as times changed, the people might need to amend the Constitution. The amendment process was used almost immediately. It was hard to get the Constitution ratified and James Madison and other Federalists wanted to get the document accepted as quickly as possible. Some states were talking about starting all over again and rewriting the document from scratch! James Madison definitely didn't want that to happen. He agreed that if the states would ratify the Constitution the way it was, he would try to get a Bill of Rights added later. And he did. (See page 105.)

Article VI.

Article VI talks about the legitimacy of the new government, including its debt, and that the national government is superior to the states.

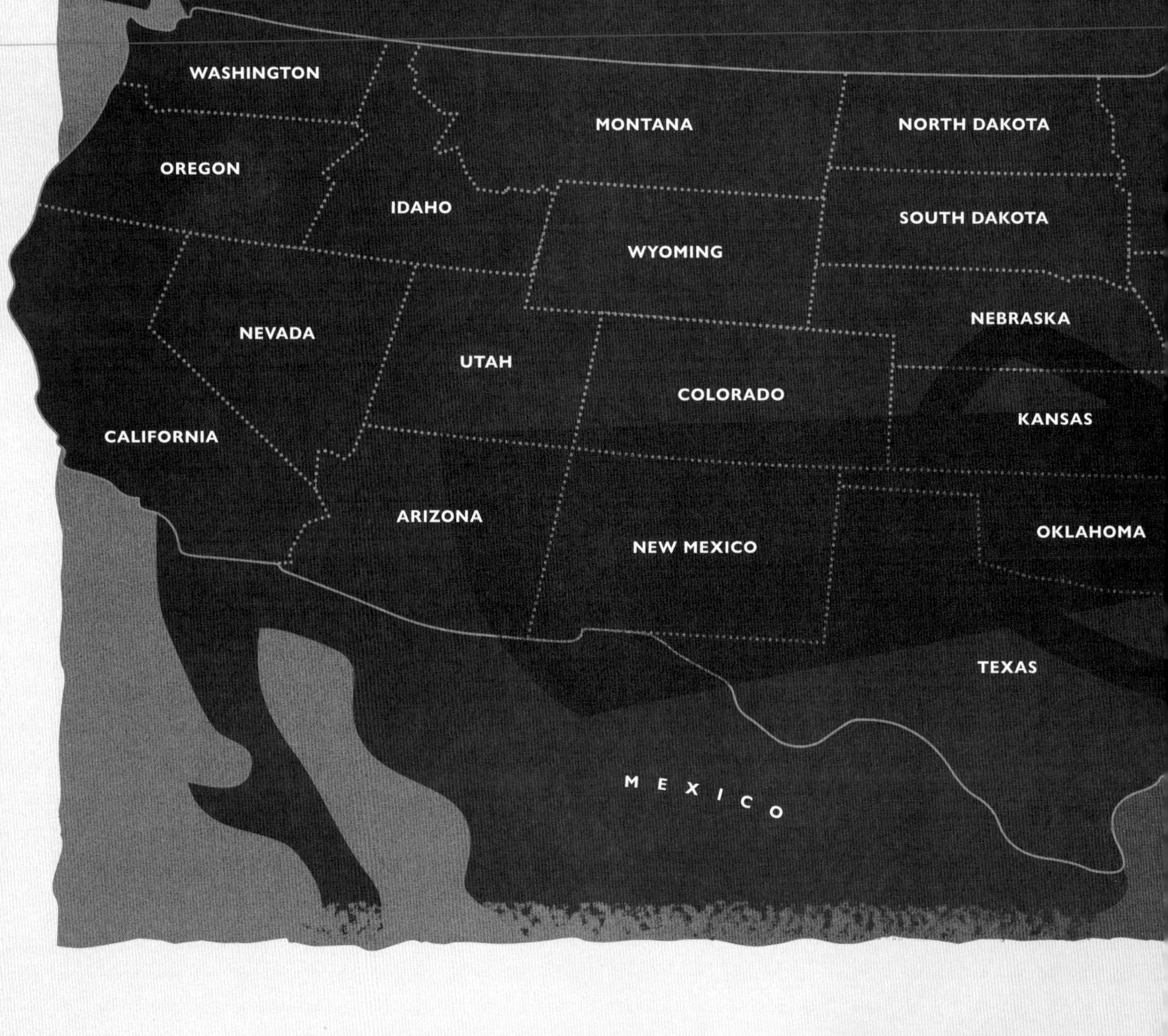

WASHINGTON

OREGON

IDAHO

MONTANA

NORTH DAKOTA

SOUTH DAKOTA

WYOMING

NEVADA

UTAH

COLORADO

NEBRASKA

KANSAS

CALIFORNIA

ARIZONA

NEW MEXICO

OKLAHOMA

TEXAS

M E X I C O

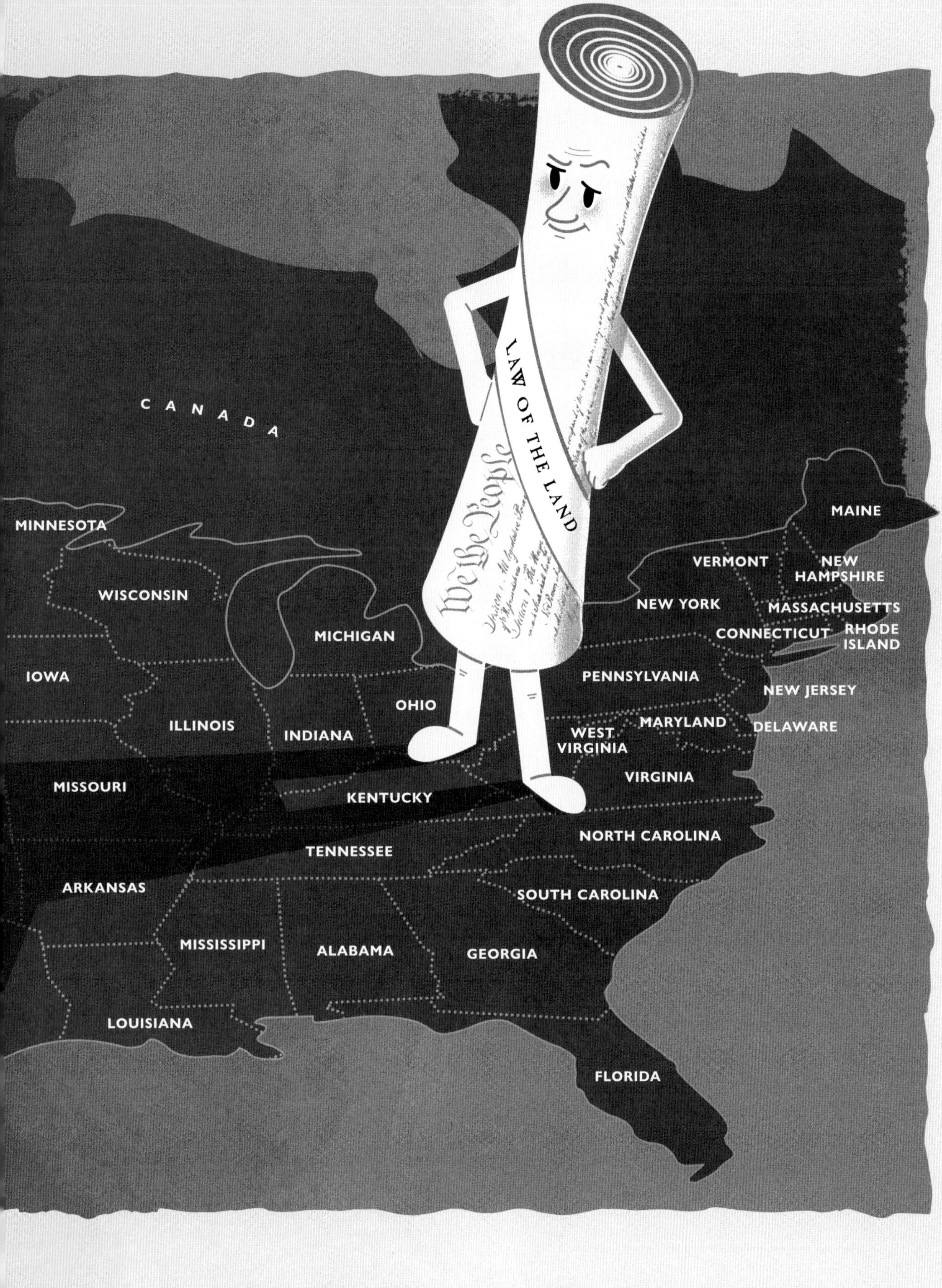

LAW OF THE LAND
We the People
CANADA
MINNESOTA
WISCONSIN
MICHIGAN
IOWA
ILLINOIS
INDIANA
OHIO
PENNSYLVANIA
NEW YORK
VERMONT
NEW HAMPSHIRE
MAINE
MASSACHUSETTS
CONNECTICUT
RHODE ISLAND
NEW JERSEY
DELAWARE
MARYLAND
WEST VIRGINIA
VIRGINIA
KENTUCKY
MISSOURI
TENNESSEE
NORTH CAROLINA
SOUTH CAROLINA
ARKANSAS
MISSISSIPPI
ALABAMA
GEORGIA
LOUISIANA
FLORIDA

ORIGINAL TEXT

All Debts contracted and Engagements entered into, before the Adoption of this Constitution, shall be as valid against the United States under this Constitution, as under the Confederation ❶. This Constitution, and the Laws of the United States which shall be made in Pursuance thereof; and all Treaties made, or which shall be made, under the Authority of the United States, shall be the supreme Law of the Land ❷; and the Judges in every State shall be bound thereby, any Thing in the Constitution or Laws of any State to the Contrary notwithstanding ❸.

The Senators and Representatives before mentioned, and the Members of the several State Legislatures, and all executive and judicial Officers, both of the United States and of the several States, shall be bound by Oath or Affirmation, to support this Constitution ❹; but no religious Test shall ever be required as a Qualification to any Office or public Trust under the United States ❺.

DID YOU KNOW?

There are fifty states, and each state has its own legislature made up of two chambers—except for Nebraska, which has a one-chamber legislature and calls its members "senators." A state legislature makes laws that apply within its own state. State laws can give people more rights than they have at the federal level but can't take away any federal rights. State laws apply to visitors to a state, too, because of the Privileges and Immunities Clause in Article IV, Section 2 (see page 84).

DEBTS WILL BE PAID!

TRANSLATION

1. All the money owed by the federal government, and all the contracts it has agreed to, before this Constitution becomes the law will still be paid by the federal government under this agreement, as they would have been paid under the previous rules.

2. This Constitution and the laws of the federal government that will be made under its guidance, and all the agreements with other countries that have been, or will be, made under the authority of the federal government, will be the highest law of the land,

3. and state judges have to enforce federal laws, no matter what their state constitutions or laws say.

4. Federal and state legislators and people in the executive and judicial branches of both federal and state governments will take an oath to uphold this Constitution,

5. and religious views will never be used to decide if someone can have a job or assignment in the federal government.

LAW OF THE LAND!

CONTRACTS HONORED!

CONSTITUTION IN ACTION

SUPREMACY CLAUSE

The Supremacy Clause in Article VI says that the federal Constitution, laws, and treaties are superior to anything else. Nothing (such as a state law or constitution) can override them.

Until the Civil War, the biggest test of the Supremacy Clause was the Nullification Crisis of 1832–33. South Carolina claimed that it had the right to nullify, or ignore, federal laws. It also said that it might secede from the Union and threatened to use force. President Andrew Jackson said that was treason. South Carolina backed down.

Article VII.

Article VII explains the ratification process
(how the states would agree to the Constitution).

The **Ratification** of the Conventions of nine States, shall be sufficient for the Establishment of this Constitution between the States so ratifying the Same ❶.

Done in Convention by the Unanimous Consent of the States present the Seventeenth Day of September in the Year of our Lord one thousand seven hundred and Eighty seven and of the Independence of the United States of America the Twelfth. In Witness whereof We have hereunto subscribed our Names.

G°. Washington—President and deputy from Virginia

New Hampshire—John Langdon, Nicholas Gilman

Massachusetts—Nathaniel Gorham, Rufus King

Connecticut—Wm. Saml. Johnson, Roger Sherman

New York—Alexander Hamilton

New Jersey—Wil: Livingston, David Brearley, Wm. Paterson, Jona: Dayton

Pennsylvania—B Franklin, Thomas Mifflin, Robt. Morris, Geo. Clymer, Thos. FitzSimons, Jared Ingersoll, James Wilson, Gouv Morris

Delaware—Geo: Read, Gunning Bedford jun, John Dickinson, Richard Bassett, Jaco: Broom

Maryland—James McHenry, Dan of St Thos. Jenifer, Danl. Carroll

Virginia—John Blair, James Madison Jr.

North Carolina—Wm. Blount, Richd. Dobbs Spaight, Hu Williamson

South Carolina—J. Rutledge, Charles Cotesworth Pinckney, Charles Pinckney, Pierce Butler

Georgia—William Few, Abr Baldwin

Attest: William Jackson, Secretary

THE ORIGINAL 13 STATES IN ORDER OF RATIFICATION OF THE US CONSTITUTION

Delaware—December 7, 1787
Pennsylvania—December 12, 1787
New Jersey—December 18, 1787
Georgia—January 2, 1788
Connecticut—January 9, 1788
Massachusetts—February 6, 1788
Maryland—April 28, 1788

South Carolina—May 23, 1788
New Hampshire—June 21, 1788
Virginia—June 25, 1788
New York—July 26, 1788
North Carolina—November 21, 1789
Rhode Island—May 29, 1790

ARTICLE VII.

1 Ratification by nine states will make the Constitution go into effect for those states that ratified it.

DID YOU KNOW?

For the Constitution to become law, nine states had to ratify it, and they did. But Rhode Island rejected it, and North Carolina, Virginia, and New York held out. The new nation needed Virginia and New York to join. Without Virginia, the United States would be split in two pieces, and the country needed New York City's harbor.

People who wanted to ratify the Constitution were called Federalists, and people who opposed it were Anti-Federalists. James Madison, who had done more than anyone else to write the document, was from Virginia, and so was George Washington, whom everyone expected to be the first president. Both men were embarrassed to think their state wouldn't join the new country. When Federalists promised to add a Bill of Rights to the Constitution, Virginia ratified the document.

Madison helped Federalists Alexander Hamilton and John Jay convince New York to ratify. Hamilton, Madison, and Jay wrote newspaper essays under a fake name, Publius, saying why they thought New York should accept the Constitution. They wrote eighty-five essays that were published together in 1788 as *The Federalist*. For all their hard work, what really got New York to ratify was New York City's threat to leave the state if it didn't. That would have made it hard for upstate farmers to get their crops to market.

The Constitution went into effect on March 4, 1789.

CONSTITUTION IN ACTION

SLAVERY

The Fugitive Slave Clause (Article IV, Section 2) was proposed by delegates from Georgia, South Carolina, and North Carolina. They wanted it to be included as the price of their support for ratification of the Constitution. Northern delegates, who at first opposed the Fugitive Slave Clause, gave in. Delegates from free states thought that preserving slavery was the price they had to pay to get the Constitution ratified—and so they agreed to it.

Vocabulary

RATIFICATION—agreement to put a document into effect

Amendments

Amendments are changes to the Constitution. An amendment counts just as much as the original document.

CONSTITUTION IN ACTION

THE BILL OF RIGHTS

The first ten amendments are known as the Bill of Rights and contain protection for basic freedoms like freedom of speech and the press. Many Anti-Federalists had opposed the Constitution because it didn't include the liberties they'd fought Great Britain to get. James Madison didn't think they were necessary and worried that any list of rights would be incomplete. Would that mean that people would *lose* rights the Framers didn't think to list? If that happened, a Bill of Rights could actually limit people's liberty, not secure it. But adding specific freedoms to the Constitution was very popular. Madison agreed to write a Bill of Rights—and it helped him win a close congressional race against James Monroe.

Madison wanted to put changes to the Constitution in their logical place in the original document. The amendments in the Bill of Rights are in the order they would have been in to slip them into the original articles, but Madison lost the argument about where to place them to Roger Sherman of Connecticut, so amendments are listed at the end of the Constitution.

DID YOU KNOW?

James Madison suggested twelve amendments, but in 1791, only ten were ratified. One of the other two proposed amendments said that Congress couldn't vote itself a pay raise. (Any raise would start with the next Congress.) That eventually became the 27th Amendment. The second proposal that didn't make it in 1791 would have decided how many members the House of Representatives should have, based on the population at that time. It wouldn't have been very practical today.

AMENDMENT I

Congress shall make no law respecting an establishment of religion, or prohibiting the free exercise thereof ❶; or abridging the freedom of speech, or of the press ❷; or the right of the people peaceably to assemble, and to petition the Government for a redress of grievances ❸.

CONSTITUTION IN ACTION

ASSEMBLIES AND PROTESTS

Freedom of assembly is the right to gather peacefully. Along with freedom of speech, it allows people to protest things they think are wrong. Some of the well-known protests in American history include the 1886 gathering at the McCormick Reaper Works in Chicago. Police had fired on workers striking for an eight-hour workday. The next day, workers held a protest at Haymarket Square and someone threw a bomb at the police. At least eight people were killed.

In 1963, Martin Luther King Jr.'s March on Washington drew 250,000 people to the nation's capital. This was where he gave his "I Have a Dream" speech about civil rights. In 1970, at Kent State University, students gathered to protest the Vietnam War. The National Guard opened fire on them, killing four students. And on January 21, 2017, the Women's March drew people to Washington, DC, to march for women's rights in protest of Donald Trump's election as president. Protests arose in other cities as well. Altogether about four and a half million people exercised their rights to freedom of speech and assembly that day.

TRANSLATION

1. Congress won't set up an official religion or make laws to keep people from practicing their religion,

2. or limiting what people can say, or what can be printed,

3. or preventing people from gathering in peaceful groups and asking the government to fix problems.

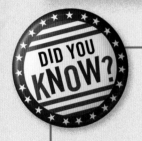

DID YOU KNOW?

Even though many colonists came to America to flee religious persecution in Europe, most colonies set up an official church in America. That meant that a sin became a crime. For example, a person might be fined by the state for skipping church. It also meant that some people had to pay taxes to support a church they didn't believe in.

Some people tried to change that. Roger Williams started the colony of Providence Plantations (part of what later became the state of Rhode Island) as a safe place for people of all religions. Maryland (in 1649) and Virginia (in 1786) passed acts of religious toleration. In 1802, Thomas Jefferson wrote about the need for "a wall of separation between church and state."

The 1st Amendment prevents Congress from setting up a national church or stopping people from following their religion. After the Civil War and the 14th Amendment, these rules were applied to states, too. But the language we often use to talk about that freedom—"separation of church and state"—doesn't actually appear in the amendment itself.

FREEDOM OF RELIGION

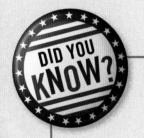

DID YOU KNOW?

The Constitution protects a citizen's right to say what they want in any form—whether it's spoken, written, printed, or expressed through action as political speech. England didn't have a tradition of freedom of speech and the press, and when the states proposed amendments during their ratification conventions, only three states suggested including freedom of speech and the press. But James Madison thought those rights were important and wrote them into the Bill of Rights.

FREEDOM OF SPEECH

DAILY NEWS

FREEDOM OF THE PRESS

ORIGINAL TEXT

AMENDMENT II

A well regulated Militia, being necessary to the security of a free State **1**, the right of the people to keep and bear Arms, shall not be infringed **2**.

DID YOU KNOW?

The United States didn't have a standing army (one that's always in place, like it has today) at the time the Constitution was written. A militia was called together when there was a threat, such as an invasion. After the threat ended, everybody went home and back to their regular jobs. The Framers also thought that states could call up their militias if the federal government became a threat to the rights of citizens, or if there was a rebellion in the state.

ORIGINAL TEXT

AMENDMENT III

No Soldier shall, in time of peace be quartered in any house, without the consent of the Owner **1**, nor in time of war, but in a manner to be prescribed by law **2**.

DID YOU KNOW?

Before the American Revolution, the English Parliament passed the Quartering Act. It made Americans provide food and shelter for British troops in the colonies, and it forced them to let soldiers into their own homes. Colonists were outraged, and when the first amendments were added to the Constitution, they included a ban on having soldiers sleep in private homes. Soldiers don't show up unannounced to live in your house anymore—and you can thank the Constitution for that.

1. Because a well-supervised militia is necessary to keep a country safe,

2. the right of the people to own and carry guns will not be limited.

1. No soldiers in peacetime will be housed in a private home without the permission of the owner,

2. or during wartime, except according to the laws.

CONSTITUTION IN ACTION

PRIVACY

The Supreme Court has never had to rule something unconstitutional based on the 3rd Amendment. But it does help establish a right to privacy, a right that is recognized today but isn't specifically listed in the Constitution.

AMENDMENT IV

The right of the people to be secure in their persons, houses, papers, and effects, against unreasonable searches and seizures, shall not be violated **1**, and no Warrants shall issue, but upon probable cause, supported by Oath or affirmation **2**, and particularly describing the place to be searched, and the persons or things to be seized **3**.

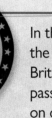

In the years before the Revolution, the British Parliament passed several taxes on colonial trade. The colonists responded by smuggling goods to avoid the taxes when they could. The British fought the smuggling with "writs of assistance" or general search warrants that allowed British officials to search buildings without having to say where they were going to go. The writs made the colonists angry. So when the Framers were adding amendments to the Constitution, it was easy to think of including warrants and requiring them to make clear exactly what could be searched and seized.

1. People and their houses, papers, and belongings are protected from being searched or taken without good reason,

2. and no document allowing a search will be given out without a reasonable belief that someone committed a crime, and that belief must be supported by an oath,

3. and the document allowing a search must be specific about the place to be searched and the people or things to be taken.

CONSTITUTION IN ACTION

WARRANTS

Warrants are court orders allowing police to search a place or take people or things into custody. Police can't search on a hunch—they need probable cause that a crime has been committed. The warrant is specific about the place that will be searched and what officers are looking for, and it must be signed by a judge.

There are some cases in which police don't need a search warrant—for example, if a person says it's okay to search their house or car, if something is in plain view, or if the time it would take to get a warrant could result in harm to the public.

AMENDMENT V

No person shall be held to answer for a capital, or otherwise infamous crime, unless on a presentment or indictment of a Grand Jury, except in cases arising in the land or naval forces, or in the Militia, when in actual service in time of War or public danger **1**; nor shall any person be subject for the same offense to be twice put in jeopardy of life or limb; nor shall be compelled in any criminal case to be a witness against himself **2**, nor be deprived of life, liberty, or property, without due process of law **3**; nor shall private property be taken for public use, without just compensation **4**.

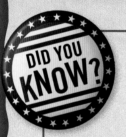

DID YOU KNOW?

Grand juries decide if there's enough evidence that a person committed a crime and that the case should go to trial. They don't decide if the person is guilty or not—that's done by the trial itself. Grand juries are made up of regular people, so it's not just government officials deciding whether to try a person. They were one of the ways to protect people from unfair government actions. More people are on a grand jury than a regular trial jury. That's why it's called "grand." In this case it means "big."

1. No one can be tried for a crime that's punishable by death unless a grand jury says so, except for active-duty military personnel (at any time) or members of a militia serving during a war or threat to public safety,

2. and no person will be tried twice for the same crime, or forced to say things that could be used against them in court,

3. or have their life, freedom, or possessions taken away without going through proper legal procedures,

4. or have their private land or possessions taken for public use without being paid a fair price.

CONSTITUTION IN ACTION

DOUBLE JEOPARDY

"Jeopardy" means danger—in this case, danger of punishment for committing a crime. The Constitution doesn't allow double jeopardy—being tried twice for the same crime—because that could be used unfairly to punish a person. If the government wanted to cause problems for someone, as soon as one trial was over it could charge the person again, making them sit through another trial and keeping them from their job and other responsibilities. If the government had the power to charge and try someone over and over, that could be used as a punishment against a person who had committed no crime.

DUE PROCESS

Requiring the government to go through proper procedures to take away a person's life, liberty, or property might seem like it only limits *how* the government can do things, not *what* it can do. But, like the Due Process Clause of the 14th Amendment (see page 132), the Due Process Clause of the 5th Amendment has also been read to protect certain fundamental rights that aren't listed in the Constitution. The government can't take these rights away no matter how it tries. Also, the 5th Amendment Due Process Clause stops the federal government from discriminating unfairly (treating people unequally without a good reason).

CAPITAL CRIMES

Capital crimes are crimes for which a person may be executed as a punishment. What counts as a capital crime has changed over time, but generally they're murders of various types, spying for another country, and treason.

AMENDMENT VI

In all criminal prosecutions, the accused shall enjoy the right to a speedy and public trial **1**, by an **impartial** jury of the State and district wherein the crime shall have been committed, which district shall have been previously ascertained by law **2**, and to be informed of the nature and cause of the accusation **3**; to be confronted with the witnesses against him **4**; to have compulsory process for obtaining witnesses in his favor **5**, and to have the Assistance of Counsel for his defence **6**.

CONSTITUTION IN ACTION

ZONE OF DEATH

The 6th Amendment says that juries have to be from the state and district where the crime was committed. But there's a part of Idaho that's in Yellowstone National Park, where no one lives. Michigan State University law professor Brian Kalt points out that no jury could be put together from that district. If you committed a crime in the Idaho part of Yellowstone Park, there's no way to form a legal jury for a trial. What's more, you couldn't be tried under state law because the states gave up their rights to govern in Yellowstone when it became a national park. So the 6th Amendment accidentally creates a fifty-square-mile area where you could commit a murder and never go to trial.

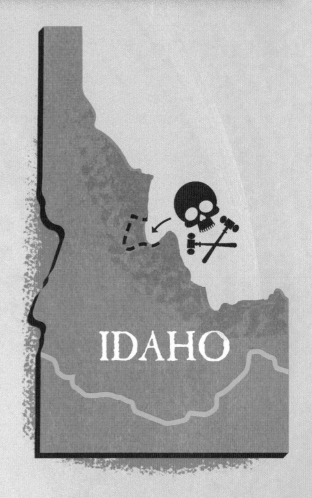

IDAHO

Vocabulary

IMPARTIAL—fair; not favoring one side or the other

TRANSLATION

1. Whenever someone's charged with a crime, the accused person is entitled to a trial to be held soon and in public,

2. with a fair jury from the state and district where the crime was committed, with the district having been determined by law ahead of the trial,

3. and the accused person will be told what crime they're charged with and the reason they're being accused

4. and has the right to face the witnesses who speak against them,

5. to force any witnesses who could help them to come to court,

6. and to have the help of a lawyer to defend them.

DID YOU KNOW?

Trial by jury is the only right mentioned in both the original Constitution and the amendments. The 6th Amendment contains guarantees to help people get a fair trial. Americans already had the right to a jury trial (except in impeachments) under Article III, but the 6th Amendment extends those protections.

A public trial makes sure that people know what the government is doing and can make sure it's being fair. A speedy trial means that people accused of crimes won't have to wait for years—sometimes in jail—before getting a chance to show they didn't do it. And holding the trial where the crime happened prevents abuses, like Britain's practice of shipping colonists to England for trial.

People get to have a lawyer to help them, too. In the 1930s, the Supreme Court said that this doesn't just mean that people are allowed to hire their own lawyers. It said that in federal trials, the government must provide a lawyer for people who can't afford one. And in 1963, the Supreme Court ruled that the 14th Amendment requires a lawyer to be provided to people on trial in state courts as well as in federal courts.

The Public

Lawyers Available

ORIGINAL TEXT

AMENDMENT VII

In Suits at **common law**, where the value in controversy shall exceed twenty dollars, the right of trial by jury shall be preserved **1**, and no fact tried by a jury, shall be otherwise re-examined in any Court of the United States, than according to the rules of the common law **2**.

Vocabulary

COMMON LAW—The idea of common law comes from England, and it is called "common" because it's the same from place to place. It was based on custom and precedent— how cases of the same type had been decided before—rather than on written law. The United States borrowed some of its law from English common law.

TRANSLATION

1. In federal lawsuits when more than twenty dollars is at stake, people keep the right to a trial by jury if they would have had it before the Constitution,

2. and no facts decided by a jury can be reviewed in any federal court, except by following any current laws about it.

DID YOU KNOW?

The 7th Amendment guarantees the right to a jury trial in some federal court cases. Civil suits are cases that don't involve crimes. Examples include disagreements about what a contract says, whether or not one person owes another person money, or if a landlord or person who rents from them isn't doing what they're supposed to. If a person loses a civil case, they might have to pay a fine or give up property that people were arguing over, but they won't go to jail.

CONSTITUTION IN ACTION

RETRYING FACTS

The 7th Amendment says that "no fact tried by a jury, shall be otherwise re-examined in any Court." "Fact" here means the details of the case: who did what to whom. If judges could look at the facts again, they could change what a jury had decided—and if they did that, the right to trial by jury wouldn't have any meaning.

ORIGINAL TEXT

AMENDMENT VIII

Excessive **bail** shall not be required **1**, nor excessive fines imposed, nor cruel and unusual punishments inflicted **2**.

DID YOU KNOW?

When Congress was debating what became the 8th Amendment, New Hampshire Representative Samuel Livermore complained about the "cruel and unusual" phrase. He said, "Villains often deserve whipping, and perhaps having their ears cut off; but are we in [the] future to be prevented from inflicting these punishments because they are cruel?" The answer was yes. Today, no one's ears are cut off—although a person might still be executed.

Vocabulary

BAIL—letting a person charged with a crime stay out of jail until their trial, often after they leave money with the court to guarantee that they'll show up

TRANSLATION

1. The amount of money an accused person leaves with the court to make sure that they show up for trial, which allows them to stay out of jail until the trial starts, can't be more than is necessary,

2. and no unreasonable fines or any cruel and uncommon punishment will be allowed.

CONSTITUTION IN ACTION

BAIL

When people accused of a crime pay bail, they don't have to stay in jail until their trial. This is a way of keeping innocent people out of jail. But if the amount required is extremely high, the system wouldn't work because people couldn't pay it.

In 2019, the Supreme Court ruled that the 8th Amendment's protection from excessive fines also protects people at the state and local levels.

The Court used the 14th Amendment to say that states can't violate the rights that the Bill of Rights gave people on the federal level.

The Supreme Court has ruled that what counts as a "cruel and unusual" punishment will change with the times. So today, whipping someone would not be allowed, even though it was once a common punishment. Some people feel that the death penalty (capital punishment) should be illegal under the 8th Amendment. Others don't. The United States currently still executes some prisoners.

ORIGINAL TEXT

AMENDMENT IX

The enumeration in the Constitution, of certain rights, shall not be construed to deny or disparage others retained by the people **1**.

CONSTITUTION IN ACTION

PRIVACY

People disagree on the meaning of the 9th Amendment. The courts haven't used it very often to decide cases, although it has been used with other amendments, like the 3rd, to establish a right to privacy.

DID YOU KNOW?

One danger with listing specific rights in the Constitution was the possibility that any freedoms the Framers forgot to include would be considered unprotected. Did people have *only* the rights listed? In his first draft of what became the 9th Amendment, James Madison said that the Bill of Rights would not limit other unlisted freedoms and that it would not expand the power of the federal government. The final version took out the line about not expanding federal power.

Some people think that the 9th Amendment is meant to limit the federal government, not to protect extra rights. Others believe that the amendment means precisely what it says—that people have other freedoms beyond those specifically listed. How to identify those "unenumerated rights" is a question people have struggled with for years.

1 Listing some specific rights in the Constitution doesn't mean people don't have other rights, too.

OTHER FREEDOMS

AMENDMENT X

The powers not delegated to the United States by the Constitution **1**, nor prohibited by it to the States **2**, are reserved to the States respectively, or to the people **3**.

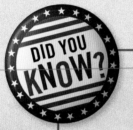

DID YOU KNOW?

The 10th Amendment didn't change anything in the Constitution. The 1st Amendment, for example, safeguarded freedom of speech and the press. But there is no specific right of the people or power of the government that the 10th Amendment grants or takes away. The last amendment in the Bill of Rights was meant to reinforce the power of the people and of the states, but it is so vague that it hasn't been used very much.

TRANSLATION

1. The authority not given to the federal government by the Constitution,
2. or taken from the states by the Constitution,
3. belongs to the individual states, or to the people.

AMENDMENT XI
RATIFIED 2/7/1795

The Judicial power of the United States shall not be construed to extend to any suit in law or equity, commenced or prosecuted against one of the United States by Citizens of another State, or by Citizens or Subjects of any Foreign State **1**.

DID YOU KNOW?

LOOK BACK

The 11th Amendment says that federal courts can't hear cases where citizens of one state (or foreign country) sue a different state. This changed part of Article III, Section 2 (see page 74).

Many people felt that the original wording of Article III interfered unfairly with state authority. After a South Carolina citizen successfully sued the state of Georgia, the 11th Amendment was quickly written to protect states from being sued in federal court. This protection from being sued is called "sovereign immunity." (A state government is a sovereign government, and it can't be sued without its consent.) The Supreme Court has said that Congress can overcome state sovereign immunity to let individuals sue states if it is doing so in order to enforce the 14th Amendment (see page 132).

1. Federal courts will not hear lawsuits where a citizen of one state or of a foreign country sues another state.

AMENDMENT XII
RATIFIED 6/15/1804

The Electors shall meet in their respective states and vote by ballot for President and Vice-President, one of whom, at least, shall not be an inhabitant of the same state with themselves ❶; they shall name in their ballots the person voted for as President, and in distinct ballots the person voted for as Vice-President ❷, and they shall make distinct lists of all persons voted for as President, and of all persons voted for as Vice-President, and of the number of votes for each, which lists they shall sign and certify, and transmit sealed to the seat of the government of the United States, directed to the President of the Senate ❸; The President of the Senate shall, in the presence of the Senate and House of Representatives, open all the certificates and the votes shall then be counted ❹;

DID YOU KNOW?

LOOK BACK

The 12th Amendment details how the president and vice president are elected, changing Article II, Section 1 (see page 50). At the time the Constitution was written, the United States didn't have political parties and the Framers didn't think it would. The original document says that whoever gets the second-highest vote total becomes vice president, but once political parties developed, that meant the president and vice president would be from different parties. Part of the 12th Amendment itself is changed by the 20th Amendment (see page 148).

VOTE

☒ PRESIDENT

☐ VICE PRESIDENT

TRANSLATION

1. The electors will meet in their own states and vote by ballot for president and vice president, and at least one of them has to be from a different state than the elector;

2. their ballots have to make it clear which person is chosen as president and which as vice president,

3. and they'll make a list of all the people who got votes for president and all the people who got votes for vice president, and how many votes each person got, and then sign, confirm, and send the sealed documents to Washington, DC, for the vice president (who is also the president of the Senate).

4. The vice president, in front of both houses of Congress, will open the lists and count the votes.

The person having the greatest number of votes for President, shall be the President, if such number be a majority of the whole number of Electors appointed **5**; and if no person have such majority, then from the persons having the highest numbers not exceeding three on the list of those voted for as President, the House of Representatives shall choose immediately, by ballot, the President **6**. But in choosing the President, the votes shall be taken by states, the representation from each state having one vote; a quorum for this purpose shall consist of a member or members from two-thirds of the states, and a majority of all the states shall be necessary to a choice **7**. And if the House of Representatives shall not choose a President whenever the right of choice shall devolve upon them, before the [fourth day of March] next following, then the Vice-President shall act as President, as in the case of the death or other constitutional disability of the President **8**. *(Note: Bracketed text was superseded by the 20th Amendment **9**.)*

The person having the greatest number of votes as Vice-President, shall be the Vice-President, if such number be a majority of the whole number of Electors appointed, and if no person have a majority, then from the two highest numbers on the list, the Senate shall choose the Vice-President; a quorum for the purpose shall consist of two-thirds of the whole number of Senators, and a majority of the whole number shall be necessary to a choice **10**. But no person **constitutionally ineligible** to the office of President shall be eligible to that of Vice-President of the United States **11**.

Vocabulary

CONSTITUTIONALLY INELIGIBLE— unable to become president because a person doesn't meet the requirements to be president listed in Article II of the Constitution

TRANSLATION

5 The person who gets the most votes for president becomes the president, as long as a majority of all the electors voted for that person.

6 If no one gets a majority of all the votes, then the House of Representatives will take a ballot vote to choose the president from among the top three.

7 In selecting the president, the vote is taken by state, and each state gets one vote; a quorum will be made up of members from two-thirds of the states, and a candidate needs a majority of all the states in order to win.

8 If the House is supposed to choose the president but hasn't before [March 4] of the year after the election, then the vice president acts as president, just as if the president had died or was unable to do the job.

9 Note: Bracketed text changed by the 20th Amendment, Section 1.* See page 148.

Changed so that the starting date for the president's and vice president's terms is not March 4 but January 20.

10 The person who gets the most votes for vice president becomes the vice president, as long as a majority of all the electors voted for them, and if no one gets a majority of all the votes, then the Senate will choose between the two people who got the most votes; a quorum will be made up of two-thirds of all the senators, and a candidate needs a majority of all the senators' votes to win.

11 No one can be the vice president if they don't meet the requirements to be president.

CONSTITUTION IN ACTION

PRESIDENT OR VICE PRESIDENT

In 1800, Thomas Jefferson ran for president with Aaron Burr as his vice president. The ballots didn't say who was running for which office, so they wound up tied. Jefferson expected Burr to give up one of his votes to make Jefferson president, but he didn't. Ties are decided in the House of Representatives—which took thirty-six votes before choosing Jefferson as president. In 1804, the 12th Amendment required ballots to make it clear whether a candidate was running for president or vice president so that this situation wouldn't happen again.

PRESIDENTIAL OFFICE

AMENDMENTS ★ AMENDMENT XIII

ORIGINAL TEXT

AMENDMENT XIII
RATIFIED 12/6/1865

SECTION 1. Neither slavery nor involuntary servitude, except as a punishment for crime whereof the party shall have been duly **convicted** ❶, shall exist within the United States, or any place subject to their jurisdiction ❷.

SECTION 2. Congress shall have power to enforce this article by appropriate legislation ❸.

The 13th Amendment was the first of three post–Civil War amendments dealing with the rights of African Americans. The 13th ended slavery; the 14th made African Americans citizens; the 15th gave African American men the right to vote.

FREDERICK DOUGLASS

TRANSLATION

① Slavery is banned, and no one can be forced to work against his or her will except as punishment for a crime for which that person was found guilty.

② This will be the case in the whole United States or any place it controls.

③ Congress has the authority to make laws to make this happen.

Mississippi

2013

DID YOU KNOW?

The last state to ratify the 13th Amendment was Mississippi—in 2013. It ratified the amendment in 1995 but didn't record the vote at that time. Mississippi's ratification became official eighteen years later—more than 147 years after the amendment took effect.

LOOK BACK

The 13th Amendment ended slavery. The Constitution didn't establish slavery—it already existed—but it did talk about it in several places. Article I, Section 2 counted a slave as three-fifths of a person when counting the population to determine how many representatives each state gets. Article I, Section 9 said that Congress couldn't ban the international slave trade before 1808. And Article IV, Section 2 said that runaway slaves will be returned to their masters.

Vocabulary

CONVICTED—found guilty of doing something illegal (a crime)

ORIGINAL TEXT

AMENDMENT XIV
RATIFIED 7/9/1868

SECTION 1. All persons born or naturalized in the United States, and subject to the jurisdiction thereof, are citizens of the United States and of the State wherein they reside **1**. No State shall make or enforce any law which shall abridge the privileges or immunities of citizens of the United States **2**; nor shall any State deprive any person of life, liberty, or property, without due process of law **3**; nor deny to any person within its jurisdiction the equal protection of the laws **4**.

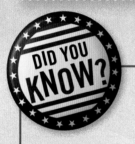

DID YOU KNOW?

The freedoms in the Bill of Rights protect Americans from actions by the federal government. The 14th Amendment protects them from having their rights violated by the *states*. The Framers worried mostly about the federal government and thought that the states would protect their citizens. That turned out to not be true, especially once Blacks became citizens under the 14th Amendment. (The first sentence of the 14th Amendment overrules the *Dred Scott* decision.) That's why the 14th Amendment requires *states* to recognize people's rights. All citizens, of any race, whether born in the United States or immigrants who become citizens, are covered by its protections. And when the amendment says "person," not citizen, it protects noncitizens, too. Many Court decisions giving people rights, like privacy, that aren't spelled out in the Constitution are based on the 14th Amendment's Due Process Clause. Other decisions giving people equal rights are based on the 14th Amendment's Equal Protection Clause (". . . nor deny to any person within its jurisdiction the equal protection of the laws"). Both these clauses protect all persons. The 14th Amendment is one of the most important parts of the Constitution. It made a fundamental change in the relationship between the states, the national government, and the people.

HARRIET TUBMAN

TRANSLATION

1. All people who are born in the United States, or who become citizens of the United States, and are governed by its laws, are citizens of the United States and of the state they live in.

2. No state can make a law that limits the rights or protections of US citizens,

3. and no state can take away a person's life, freedom, or possessions without going through the proper procedures

4. or treat people differently without a good enough reason.

CONSTITUTION IN ACTION

DUE PROCESS

The 14th Amendment says that states can't take away a person's "life, liberty, or property, without due process of law." This is the Due Process Clause. Thomas Jefferson's words in the Declaration of Independence—that life, liberty, and the pursuit of happiness are basic rights—had no force of law. The Due Process Clause in the Constitution protects these freedoms and has been the basis of a wide range of court decisions, including those protecting the right to travel and the right to privacy.

US Citizenship and Immigration Services

ORIGINAL TEXT

SECTION 2. Representatives shall be apportioned among the several States according to their respective numbers, counting the whole number of persons in each State, excluding Indians not taxed ❺. But when the right to vote at any election for the choice of electors for President and Vice-President of the United States, Representatives in Congress, the Executive and Judicial officers of a State, or the members of the Legislature thereof, is denied to any of the male inhabitants of such State, being [twenty-one years of age ❻] *(Note: Bracketed text changed by the 26th Amendment ❼)*, and citizens of the United States, or in any way abridged, except for participation in rebellion, or other crime, the basis of representation therein shall be reduced in the proportion which the number of such male citizens shall bear to the whole number of male citizens twenty-one years of age in such State ❽.

DID YOU KNOW?

The 14th Amendment makes anyone born in the United States a citizen—except Native Americans, who had to wait more than fifty years to have their citizenship recognized. Natives who lived on tribal land and kept their traditional cultural identity were considered "untaxed Indians" and weren't eligible for citizenship. Their citizenship status was unclear until 1924, when the Indian Citizenship Act said that Native Americans, too, were United States citizens. Even then, some states tried to prevent them from voting.

RICHARD OAKES

TRANSLATION

5 The number of representatives a state gets will be based on its population by counting all the people in the state, except Native Americans who are not taxed.

6 But when the right to vote in federal or state elections is taken away from any of the men in a state who are at least [twenty-one years old]

7 Note: Bracketed text changed by the 26th Amendment, Section 1.★ See page 166.

Changed so that the voting age is eighteen.

8 and are citizens of the United States, or is limited in any way, except if they participated in rebellion or another crime, the state's representation will be reduced by the percentage of eligible voters who weren't allowed to vote.

ORIGINAL TEXT

SECTION 3. No person shall be a Senator or Representative in Congress, or elector of President and Vice-President, or hold any office, civil or military, under the United States, or under any State, who, having previously taken an oath, as a member of Congress, or as an officer of the United States, or as a member of any State legislature, or as an executive or judicial officer of any State, to support the Constitution of the United States, shall have engaged in insurrection or rebellion against the same, or given aid or comfort to the enemies thereof **9**. But Congress may by a vote of two-thirds of each House, remove such disability **10**.

SECTION 4. The validity of the public debt of the United States, authorized by law, including debts incurred for payment of **pensions** and bounties for services in suppressing insurrection or rebellion, shall not be questioned **11**. But neither the United States nor any State shall assume or pay any debt or obligation incurred in aid of insurrection or rebellion against the United States **12**, or any claim for the loss or emancipation of any slave **13**; but all such debts, obligations and claims shall be held illegal and void **14**.

SECTION 5. The Congress shall have power to enforce, by appropriate legislation, the provisions of this article **15**.

Vocabulary

PENSION—money that an employer pays its workers on a regular basis after they've retired

(9) No person will be a senator or representative, an elector for president or vice president, or a military officer or hold any office in the federal government or any state government if he or she took an oath to uphold and defend the Constitution as a member of Congress, an officer of the federal government, a member of a state legislature, or a governor or state judge, if they rebelled against the United States or helped its enemies,

(10) but Congress can allow that person to do so if two-thirds of both houses say it's okay.

(11) The legitimacy of the federal debt, approved by law, including debts from pensions and bonuses for helping to stop a rebellion, will not be questioned.

(12) But neither the federal government nor state governments will take on or pay any debt that came from helping a rebellion against the United States

(13) or any requests for money as compensation for the loss or freeing of any slave;

(14) all those debts are illegal and won't be paid.

(15) Congress can pass laws to make this happen.

FUNDING REBELS

HELPING ENEMIES

DEFENDING THE CONSTITUTION

AMENDMENT XV
RATIFIED 2/3/1870

SECTION 1. The right of citizens of the United States to vote shall not be denied or abridged by the United States or by any State on account of race, color, or previous condition of servitude **1**.

SECTION 2. The Congress shall have power to enforce this article by appropriate legislation **2**.

DID YOU KNOW?

The last line of the 15th Amendment—"The Congress shall have power to enforce this article by appropriate legislation"—isn't usually a very controversial line. But massive White resistance to Black voting rights led to the passage of the Voting Rights Act of 1965. Among other things, this act outlawed literacy tests and allowed federal officials to keep watch over voter registration in counties that had tried to keep Black people from voting. President Lyndon B. Johnson signed the bill, saying, "This law covers many pages, but the heart of the act is plain. Wherever . . . states and counties are using regulations, or laws, or tests to deny the right to vote, then they will be struck down."

MARTIN LUTHER KING JR.

VOTE

AMENDMENTS ★ AMENDMENT XV

TRANSLATION

1. The right of US citizens to vote won't be refused or limited by the federal government or any state government because of the citizen's race or color or because they used to be slaves.

2. Congress can write laws to enforce the 15th Amendment.

CONSTITUTION IN ACTION

GRANDFATHER CLAUSES

The 15th Amendment gave Black men the right to vote. (Black women had to wait for the 19th Amendment, which gave the right to vote to all women, see page 146.) But states tried to find ways to deny their voting rights, often with grandfather clauses. Grandfather clauses could vary slightly, but the idea was that if your older family members had been able to vote before the 15th Amendment, you were also eligible to vote and didn't have to pass the same tests as other people. It was a way to let White men vote and stop Black men from voting that didn't mention race. Grandfather clauses were a deliberate attempt by states to get around a federal guarantee of voting rights.

In addition to grandfather clauses, some states used other tests to prevent Black men (and sometimes poor Whites) from voting. Literacy tests required people to prove that they could read. Property tests required them to be rich enough to vote. For example, an 1898 Louisiana law said that no one who could vote on or before January 1, 1867, or any son or grandson of such a person (as long as they were old enough) could be denied the right to vote based on educational and property requirements. Because Black people hadn't been able to vote at the date mentioned in the law, it stopped future voting by Black men who couldn't meet the requirements —but not voting by White men.

Racial discrimination in voting was widespread and very effective until the passage of the Voting Rights Act in 1965. That act, along with the 24th Amendment and some Supreme Court decisions, made the right to vote more meaningful for Black Americans. But fights over restrictions on voting continue.

AMENDMENT XVI
RATIFIED 2/3/1913

The Congress shall have power to lay and collect taxes on incomes **1**, from whatever source derived, without apportionment among the several States **2**, and without regard to any census or enumeration **3**.

DID YOU KNOW?

One of the causes of the American Revolution was the taxes that Britain put on the American colonists. The colonists didn't think it was fair to tax them without allowing them representation in Parliament. Under the Articles of Confederation, every state had to approve a tax, making it very difficult for the federal government to raise money. The nation had to ask the states for money and hope they would send it—it couldn't make them. The states didn't always send the money necessary for the federal government to run, and when they did, it wasn't always the full amount. The Constitution gave Congress the power to tax individuals, but it said that direct taxes had to be "apportioned" among states, which means adjusted so that they were even according to population.

During the Civil War, both the Union and Confederacy started taxing incomes. The Confederate tax ended with its other laws when the South lost the Civil War. In 1872, ten years after it had put an income tax in place and seven years after the war ended, the US Congress repealed the income tax. In 1892, it enacted another one, which included a tax on passive income, but the Supreme Court ruled that it was unconstitutional. It wasn't until the 16th Amendment passed in 1913 that the government's right to tax all forms of income was firmly established.

TAX BILL PASSED

TAX BILL PASSED

TRANSLATION

1. Congress has the authority to put in and collect a tax on money that people make,

2. no matter how it was earned, without dividing it between states,

3. and without paying attention to how many people live in each state.

CONSTITUTION IN ACTION

INCOME TAX

The 16th Amendment establishes the power to impose the income tax. Article I of the Constitution required certain kinds of taxes to be divided among the states according to population. But this couldn't be done fairly with an income tax because some states have higher income per person than others. So if a tax on passive income, or money that is earned outside of work, had to be divided, as the Supreme Court had said, people couldn't be taxed at the same rate. The 16th Amendment made it possible for Congress to tax passive income, as well as the money that people earn from their jobs, without dividing the tax among the states according to population.

AMENDMENT XVII
RATIFIED 4/8/1913

The Senate of the United States shall be composed of two Senators from each State, elected by the people thereof, for six years; and each Senator shall have one vote ❶. The electors in each State shall have the qualifications requisite for electors of the most numerous branch of the State legislatures ❷.

When vacancies happen in the representation of any State in the Senate, the executive authority of such State shall issue writs of election to fill such vacancies ❸: Provided, That the legislature of any State may empower the executive thereof to make temporary appointments until the people fill the vacancies by election as the legislature may direct ❹.

This amendment shall not be so construed as to affect the election or term of any Senator chosen before it becomes valid as part of the Constitution ❺.

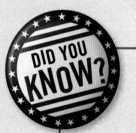

DID YOU KNOW?

The 17th Amendment was written during the Progressive Era (1890s through 1920s), a time when many people tried to make things better in the country, tackling problems like child labor and workplace safety. Some people felt that special interests had made the process of choosing senators dishonest and unfair. They thought that rich companies were getting state legislatures to pick candidates who would help them make more money instead of working for the people. The solution they chose was to let people choose their senators themselves.

TRANSLATION

1. The Senate will be made up of two senators from each state, who will be chosen by the people of the state, for a term of six years, and each senator will have one vote.

2. The voters in each state will have the qualifications required to vote for the largest house of the state legislature.

3. When a seat in the Senate is empty, the state's governor will call an election to choose a new senator,

4. and the state legislature can give the governor the authority to put someone in the job temporarily until a new senator is elected, according to the legislature's rules.

5. This amendment will not be interpreted to make any difference in the election or term of any senator who was elected before it goes into effect as part of the Constitution.

DID YOU KNOW?

LOOK BACK

Article I, Section 3 says that state legislatures elect each state's senators. The Framers were trying to balance the government, giving control of the House of Representatives to the people and of the Senate to the states. The 17th Amendment allows people to choose their own senators directly. The Progressives did this to reduce corruption. But it made senators think less about states' rights because state legislatures no longer elected them and the senators were less dependent on the states.

ORIGINAL TEXT

AMENDMENT XVIII
RATIFIED 1/16/1919
REPEALED BY AMENDMENT XXI 12/5/1933

SECTION 1. After one year from the ratification of this article ❶ the manufacture, sale, or transportation of intoxicating liquors within, the importation thereof into, or the exportation thereof from the United States and all territory subject to the jurisdiction thereof for beverage purposes is hereby prohibited ❷.

SECTION 2. The Congress and the several States shall have concurrent power to enforce this article by appropriate legislation ❸.

SECTION 3. This article shall be inoperative unless it shall have been ratified as an amendment to the Constitution by the legislatures of the several States, as provided in the Constitution, within seven years from the date of the submission hereof to the States by the Congress ❹.

BEVERAGES

TRANSLATION

1. One year after this amendment is officially included as part of the Constitution,

2. making, selling, or moving alcoholic beverages inside the United States and its territories, or bringing them into or sending them out from the country or its territories, is forbidden.

3. Congress and the states can both make laws to make this happen.

4. This amendment won't go into effect unless it's approved as an amendment to the Constitution by the state legislatures, as is laid out in the Constitution, within seven years from the date it was sent to the states by Congress.

DID YOU KNOW?

To "prohibit" something means to not allow it. The Prohibition movement tried to outlaw alcoholic drinks like wine and beer.

The history of many different kinds of Americans is caught up in Prohibition. Thousands of Irish and Germans immigrated to the United States in the 1800s. They were used to drinking alcohol in the countries they came from. For some people, the anti-alcohol campaign was a way to complain about immigrants. There was also a racist element to the drive for Prohibition. The Ku Klux Klan, an anti-Black domestic terrorist organization, was extremely powerful around the time the 18th Amendment was ratified. Klan members were often deputized to help find people producing alcohol illegally, and they used the opportunity to conduct raids without warrants on the homes of Black and immigrant Americans.

In addition, many early advocates of temperance, or not drinking too much, were women. Women formed groups to push policies they thought would help children and families—issues where their participation wasn't too controversial. Skills and connections that women made while trying to get Prohibition passed were useful as they fought to get the vote and then moved on to other issues.

ORIGINAL TEXT

AMENDMENT XIX
RATIFIED 8/18/1920

The right of citizens of the United States to vote shall not be denied or abridged by the United States or by any State on account of sex **1**.

Congress shall have power to enforce this article by appropriate legislation **2**.

DID YOU KNOW?

The Seneca Falls Convention in Seneca Falls, New York, in 1848 was the beginning of the women's rights movement in the United States. When the 15th Amendment, giving Black men the right to vote, was sent to the states for ratification, American women split. They had wanted women to be included in the amendment, and while some suffrage activists wanted the 15th Amendment to become law—with the hope that women would get the vote next—other women didn't want it to pass until they were included.

ELIZABETH CADY STANTON

TRANSLATION

1. The voting rights of US citizens will not be refused or limited by the federal government or any state government because of the citizen's sex.

2. Congress can make laws to make this happen.

CONSTITUTION IN ACTION

BLACK WOMEN'S RIGHTS

The women's rights movement also split on racial lines. Sojourner Truth gave a famous speech in 1851 known as "Ain't I a Woman?" in which she pointed out that Black women were being left out of the women's rights movement. Some Black women felt excluded from leadership roles in the struggle for suffrage and resented the attention to voting rights for Black men—but not for them. In addition, Black women faced issues that White women didn't, such as the threat of lynching. The way in which different characteristics like race and sex can overlap and interact is called "intersectionality."

SOJOURNER TRUTH

ORIGINAL TEXT

AMENDMENT XX
RATIFIED 1/23/1933

SECTION 1. The terms of the President and Vice President shall end at noon on the 20th day of January ❶, and the terms of Senators and Representatives at noon on the 3d day of January ❷, of the years in which such terms would have ended if this article had not been ratified ❸; and the terms of their successors shall then begin ❹.

SECTION 2. The Congress shall assemble at least once in every year, and such meeting shall begin at noon on the 3d day of January, unless they shall by law appoint a different day ❺.

LOOK BACK

The 20th Amendment changes the date that Article I, Section 4 (see page 24) sets for the beginning of Congress's session. It also changes the date on which the president and vice president start their jobs. The date moved from March to January so the old president and vice president don't stay in office for as long after an election. An official who isn't reelected but is still in office is called a "lame duck." He or she is still doing the people's business but is no longer accountable to the people—voters have no power to vote him or her out at that point. Giving people who have lost their position, or who did not run for reelection, several months to continue to work didn't seem wise. They wanted the newly elected officials to take over more quickly.

TRANSLATION

① The president and vice president's time in office ends at noon on January 20,

② and senators' and representatives' time in office ends at noon on January 3,

③ of the years in which their time would have ended if this article had not become part of the Constitution,

④ and the terms of the next people to do the job will begin then.

⑤ Congress has to meet at least once every year, beginning at noon on January 3, unless it passes a law to change the day.

DID YOU KNOW?

The first Congress began work on Wednesday, March 4, 1789, as the Constitution required. Because their terms were for a set length of time, the people elected to subsequent or future terms had to take over on the same date. That couldn't be changed by a law because a law can't override the Constitution, so it took a constitutional amendment to move the start-work date closer to the election that brought people into office.

AMENDMENTS ★ AMENDMENT XX (continued)

SECTION 3. If, at the time fixed for the beginning of the term of the President, the President elect shall have died, the Vice President elect shall become President **6**. If a President shall not have been chosen before the time fixed for the beginning of his term, or if the President elect shall have failed to qualify, then the Vice President elect shall act as President until a President shall have qualified **7**; and the Congress may by law provide for the case wherein neither a President elect nor a Vice President elect shall have qualified, declaring who shall then act as President, or the manner in which one who is to act shall be selected, and such person shall act accordingly until a President or Vice President shall have qualified **8**.

SECTION 4. The Congress may by law provide for the case of the death of any of the persons from whom the House of Representatives may choose a President whenever the right of choice shall have devolved upon them **9**, and for the case of the death of any of the persons from whom the Senate may choose a Vice President whenever the right of choice shall have devolved upon them **10**.

SECTION 5. Sections 1 and 2 shall take effect on the 15th day of October following the ratification of this article **11**.

SECTION 6. This article shall be inoperative unless it shall have been ratified as an amendment to the Constitution by the legislatures of three-fourths of the several States within seven years from the date of its submission **12**.

TRANSLATION

6 If, when the president is supposed to take office, the person who was elected president has died, the person who was elected to be vice president will be the president.

7 If a president hasn't been chosen before the new president is supposed to take office, or if the person who was elected doesn't qualify for the office, then the person who was elected to be vice president will do the job of president, but will not technically be the president, until a president has qualified.

8 Congress can make laws about what to do if neither the president nor the vice president has qualified for the office, including laws that say who acts as president and how that person is chosen, and that person will act as president until a new president or vice president has qualified.

9 Congress can pass laws explaining what to do if any of the people in the group from which the House of Representatives is supposed to choose the president has died, in situations where the House is making that choice,

10 and what to do if any of the people in the group from which the Senate is supposed to choose the vice president has died, in situations where the Senate is making that choice.

11 Sections 1 and 2 of this amendment take effect on October 15 after the states have agreed to put the amendment into effect.

12 This amendment is not valid unless it has been approved as an amendment to the Constitution by three-fourths of the state legislatures within seven years from the date it is sent to the states by Congress.

AMENDMENT XXI
RATIFIED 12/5/1933

SECTION 1. The eighteenth article of amendment to the Constitution of the United States is hereby **repealed** ❶.

SECTION 2. The transportation or importation into any State, Territory, or possession of the United States for delivery or use therein of intoxicating liquors, in violation of the laws thereof, is hereby prohibited ❷.

SECTION 3. This article shall be inoperative unless it shall have been ratified as an amendment to the Constitution by conventions in the several States, as provided in the Constitution, within seven years from the date of the submission hereof to the States by the Congress ❸.

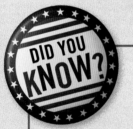

DID YOU KNOW?

Many people who had supported the 18th Amendment and had spent years trying to get Congress to pass it thought it would only ban hard liquor like whiskey. But Congress included beer and wine in the amendment, which made it much less popular. Prohibition did have some good effects: Fewer people went to the hospital because of alcohol use or died from drinking too much. But organized crime increased during the same period, and many people felt that was related to the alcohol ban. In addition, Prohibition wiped out the beer industry: The United States went from 1,300 breweries to 0 after the 18th Amendment went into effect.

When the Great Depression started in 1929, some people stopped caring as much about alcohol use. The nation had more serious problems. In 1933, the 21st Amendment repealed the 18th.

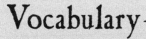

AMENDMENTS ★ AMENDMENT XXI

Vocabulary

REPEALED—overturned; canceled

1. The 18th Amendment is no longer law.

2. Moving or bringing alcoholic beverages into any state, territory, or area under the control of the United States, for supply or use, is not allowed if it's against the local laws.

3. This amendment will not go into effect unless the states agree to have it be an amendment, according to the process written in the Constitution, within seven years from the date it is sent to the states by Congress.

CONSTITUTION IN ACTION

REPEALING AN AMENDMENT

The 21st Amendment is the only amendment to undo a previous one. The 18th Amendment banned making, selling, or transporting alcohol, but the 21st Amendment overrides it, meaning that the 18th Amendment was no longer in effect once the 21st was ratified. Just by chance, the amendments that deal with alcohol have the same numbers as the ages at which states have allowed people to start drinking: eighteen and twenty-one. Not every amendment has a built-in memory aid.

AMENDMENT XXII
RATIFIED 2/27/1951

SECTION 1. No person shall be elected to the office of the President more than twice, ❶ and no person who has held the office of President, or acted as President, for more than two years of a term to which some other person was elected President shall be elected to the office of the President more than once ❷. But this Article shall not apply to any person holding the office of President, when this Article was proposed by the Congress ❸, and shall not prevent any person who may be holding the office of President, or acting as President, during the term within which this Article becomes operative from holding the office of President or acting as President during the remainder of such term ❹.

SECTION 2. This article shall be inoperative unless it shall have been ratified as an amendment to the Constitution by the legislatures of three-fourths of the several States within seven years from the date of its submission to the States by the Congress ❺.

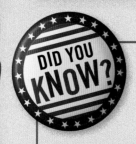

DID YOU KNOW?

George Washington strongly opposed a lifetime term for the president. He was elected twice, but he thought the act of leaving office would be as important as his service in office because it would set the example of stepping down. What's more, Washington's health was so bad that he was afraid he'd die before he got a chance to complete the second part of his service—leaving office.

1. No one can be elected president more than twice,

2. and no one who has been president, or been a substitute for a president for more than two years of someone else's term, can be elected president more than once.

3. This does not apply to anyone who is the president when this amendment is proposed,

4. and will not keep anyone who may be the president, or acting as a substitute, when this amendment goes into effect from being the president, or acting as a substitute, for the rest of their time in office.

5. This amendment will not go into effect unless it is ratified by three-fourths of the states within seven years from the date it is sent to the states by Congress.

CONSTITUTION IN ACTION

FRANKLIN ROOSEVELT

Franklin D. Roosevelt took office in 1933, early in the Great Depression. His first two terms focused on the economy. His second term ended right as another crisis was beginning— World War II. Roosevelt won a third term, and then a fourth when he ran for the last time in 1944. He died in 1945 and his vice president, Harry Truman, became president. Franklin Roosevelt was the only person elected president more than twice.

Some people felt that letting a president run for office repeatedly risked turning the office into a lifetime appointment, something the Framers specifically did not want to happen. A long-term president could also throw off the balance of power among the three branches of government. So Congress passed the 22nd Amendment, making sure that no future president could serve more than two full terms.

AMENDMENT XXIII
RATIFIED 3/29/1961

SECTION 1. The District constituting the seat of Government of the United States shall appoint in such manner as the Congress may direct ❶: A number of electors of President and Vice President equal to the whole number of Senators and Representatives in Congress to which the District would be entitled if it were a State ❷, but in no event more than the least populous State ❸; they shall be in addition to those appointed by the States, but they shall be considered, for the purposes of the election of President and Vice President, to be electors appointed by a State ❹; and they shall meet in the District and perform such duties as provided by the twelfth article of amendment ❺.
SECTION 2. The Congress shall have power to enforce this article by appropriate legislation ❻.

DID YOU KNOW?

The Constitution said that Congress could set up a ten-mile-square area to be the nation's capital. George Washington personally chose the spot that became Washington, DC, and Maryland and Virginia gave the land. Congress had met in New York City and Philadelphia but moved to Washington, DC, as a permanent home in 1800.

The choice of location became important during the Civil War, when the capital was almost surrounded by Confederate territory. Washington, DC, was in danger through most of the war, and at least once President Lincoln watched a battle with binoculars from the White House. He also came under enemy fire: Late in the war, Confederate troops attacked nearby and the commander-in-chief personally led Union troops down the road to meet them. When a Confederate sharpshooter hit a man standing beside the president, a Union soldier allegedly yelled, "Get down, you fool!" The soldier was thought to have been future Supreme Court justice Oliver Wendell Holmes Jr.

TRANSLATION

1. Washington, DC, will assign in the way that the Senate and House of Representatives set up:

2. A number of electors for president and vice president that equals the number of senators and representatives it would be allowed if it were a state,

3. but it can't have more electors than the state with the fewest people.

4. The electors from Washington, DC, are added to the electors the states have chosen, but for choosing the president and vice president they'll be seen as electors appointed by a state,

5. and they will meet in Washington, DC, to do their job according to the 12th Amendment.

6. Congress can pass laws to make this happen.

CONSTITUTION IN ACTION

WASHINGTON, DC

When the government moved to Washington, DC, in 1800, not many people lived there year-round. As the population increased, DC residents complained that they had all the responsibilities of citizenship, like being subject to the draft and paying income tax, but they had no voice in presidential elections. They had no representatives in the Electoral College. The 23rd Amendment gave DC electors, which meant their votes would count. At the time the amendment was passed, the District of Columbia had more people than thirteen states. (Its population is smaller now.) While the 23rd Amendment gave DC residents a voice in presidential elections, they still have no voting representatives in Congress. DC license plates say "end taxation without representation" as a way to protest this lack of representation.

ORIGINAL TEXT

AMENDMENT XXIV
RATIFIED 1/23/1964

SECTION 1. The right of citizens of the United States to vote in any **primary** or other election for President or Vice President, for electors for President or Vice President, or for Senator or Representative in Congress ❶, shall not be denied or abridged by the United States or any State ❷ by reason of failure to pay any **poll tax** or other tax ❸.

SECTION 2. The Congress shall have power to enforce this article by appropriate legislation ❹.

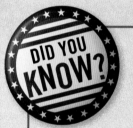

DID YOU KNOW?

After the 15th Amendment prohibited open racial discrimination in voting, many states began using tests and other hurdles to continue to restrict Black people's right to vote. The Voting Rights Act of 1965 prohibited requirements that continued discrimination. When he signed the Voting Rights Act of 1965, President Lyndon B. Johnson complained about Black voters being asked to recite the entire Constitution before they were allowed to have a ballot. This was a violation of the very document they were told to recite. Another requirement that some states used was a poll, or voting, tax. This was a way of keeping Black men, and sometimes poor White men, from voting.

The 24th Amendment says that poll taxes can't be used to prevent voting in federal elections, including the primaries (which choose the candidates who will run against each other in the general election). But it didn't say that they couldn't be used in state elections. In the Voting Rights Act, Congress declared that poll taxes in state elections were unconstitutional restrictions on the right to vote. In 1966, the Supreme Court agreed and held them unconstitutional.

The Voting Rights Act of 1965 finished what the 15th and 24th Amendments had begun—protecting people's right to vote. In 2013, the Supreme Court decided in *Shelby County v. Holder* that most of the Voting Rights Act was no longer necessary and stopped the government from enforcing it. Several states immediately enacted new restrictions on voting.

MARTIN LUTHER KING JR.

TRANSLATION

1. American citizens' right to vote in a primary or any other election for president, vice president, electors, senators, or representatives in Congress

2. will not be denied or limited by the federal government or any state government

3. because they didn't pay a fee or any other tax.

4. Congress can write laws to make this happen.

Vocabulary

PRIMARY—an election to choose who will represent a political party in the general election. A primary election is between members of the same political party.

POLL TAX—money you have to pay to vote. Poll taxes were put in place to discourage voting by Black Americans and sometimes poor Whites.

CONSTITUTION IN ACTION

VOTING FOR PRESIDENT

Voting for the president and vice president is done on a state-by-state basis, with states deciding for themselves how to run their elections. The political parties choose (or nominate) their candidates a few months before the general election, which happens in November. Some states have primaries with voting by secret ballot. Others use caucuses, where voters meet, talk about the candidates, and vote at the end of the meeting. Right now, Iowa holds the first caucus and New Hampshire has the earliest primary election. It's easier to become a party's nominee if a candidate does well in the states that vote early, so candidates visit those states often to try to win voters.

Each party has a convention, usually in late July or early August, before the general election. The parties used to pick their presidential candidate at the convention, but now they choose earlier at a nominating convention. The presidential candidate typically announces his or her running mate, the vice presidential candidate, at the convention, and the party's platform is chosen then, too. The platform is what the party stands on—what the party wants to do if it wins office.

After being chosen to represent their party, the presidential and vice presidential candidates campaign across the country, explaining to the voters what they want to accomplish. They also usually have debates with candidates from other parties.

The whole nation votes on the same day—every four years on the Tuesday following the first Monday in November, although early and absentee voting are permitted in many states. (Other elections will be held in the years between presidential elections. For example, members of the House of Representatives will run in the "midterm" elections—an election held halfway through a presidential term.) Voters cast ballots for electors, who vote in the Electoral College, even though the presidential candidate's name is usually the one on the ballot.

The electors meet in the state capitals in December and vote there, then send the results to Washington, DC, and the electoral votes are officially counted in a joint session of Congress in early January.

ORIGINAL TEXT

AMENDMENT XXV
RATIFIED 2/10/1967

SECTION 1. In case of the removal of the President from office or of his death or resignation, the Vice President shall become President ❶.

SECTION 2. Whenever there is a vacancy in the office of the Vice President, the President shall nominate a Vice President who shall take office upon confirmation by a majority vote of both Houses of Congress ❷.

SECTION 3. Whenever the President transmits to the President pro tempore of the Senate and the Speaker of the House of Representatives ❸ his written declaration that he is unable to discharge the powers and duties of his office ❹, and until he transmits to them a written declaration to the contrary ❺, such powers and duties shall be discharged by the Vice President as Acting President ❻.

CONSTITUTION IN ACTION

ACTING PRESIDENT

If the president can't do his or her job for a short time—for example, if the president is really sick—the vice president becomes acting president. The acting president has all the powers and responsibilities of the presidency—he or she does all the work—but is not technically the president and steps down when the president is able to return.

TRANSLATION

1. If the president is removed from office, dies, or steps down, the vice president will become president.

2. If there's no vice president, the president picks someone who will become vice president if the majority of the members in both the Senate and the House of Representatives agree.

3. When the president tells the leaders of the Senate and the House of Representatives

4. in writing that he cannot carry out the functions and responsibilities of his job,

5. and until he tells them in writing that he can do his job again,

6. the functions and responsibilities will be carried out by the vice president as a substitute.

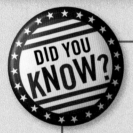

DID YOU KNOW?

The 25th Amendment makes it clear that if the president dies or is removed from office, the vice president becomes the president. But before its passage, no one was sure what to do in that situation—even though it had already come up.

President William Henry Harrison died in 1841. Was Vice President John Tyler just the acting president—or really the president? No one knew, but Tyler insisted that he was the president and everyone went along with it. After that, people agreed that a vice president who takes over is the president, not just a person doing the job until the next true president is chosen.

The 25th Amendment was passed after President John F. Kennedy was assassinated in Dallas in 1963. His vice president, Lyndon B. Johnson, took the oath of office on Air Force One. Afterward, many people worried about what might happen if a president wasn't able to do the job and there was no vice president to step in. The 25th Amendment was the result.

The amendment ensures that there will be a vice president, which is important because that person is first in line to take over. And it says what to do if the president is temporarily unable to work—or is unable to but can't or won't admit it—for example, if the president has a stroke.

Illness isn't the only reason a president might not be able to do the job. James Madison was almost captured by the British during the War of 1812. The 25th Amendment made sure that if a president becomes an enemy's prisoner, he or she can no longer give orders to the army.

ORIGINAL TEXT

SECTION 4. Whenever the Vice President and a majority of either the principal officers of the executive departments or of such other body as Congress may by law provide **7**, transmit to the President pro tempore of the Senate and the Speaker of the House of Representatives their written declaration that the President is unable to discharge the powers and duties of his office **8**, the Vice President shall immediately assume the powers and duties of the office as Acting President **9**.

Thereafter, when the President transmits to the President pro tempore of the Senate and the Speaker of the House of Representatives his written declaration that no inability exists **10**, he shall resume the powers and duties of his office unless the Vice President and a majority of either the principal officers of the executive department or of such other body as Congress may by law provide, transmit within four days to the President pro tempore of the Senate and the Speaker of the House of Representatives their written declaration that the President is unable to discharge the powers and duties of his office **11**. Thereupon Congress shall decide the issue, assembling within forty-eight hours for that purpose if not in session **12**. If the Congress, within twenty-one days after receipt of the latter written declaration, or, if Congress is not in session, within twenty-one days after Congress is required to assemble, determines by two-thirds vote of both Houses that the President is unable to discharge the powers and duties of his office, the Vice President shall continue to discharge the same as Acting President **13**; otherwise, the President shall resume the powers and duties of his office **14**.

7 If the vice president and a majority of the Cabinet, or another group that Congress sets up,

8 tell the leaders of the Senate and the House of Representatives in writing that the president cannot carry out the rights and responsibilities of his job,

9 the vice president immediately takes on the authority and responsibility of the president as a substitute.

10 Later, when the president tells the leaders of the Senate and the House of Representatives in writing that nothing prevents him from acting as president,

11 he will again take over the authority and responsibilities of the office as president unless the vice president and a majority of the Cabinet, or another group that Congress sets up, write the leaders of the Senate and the House of Representatives within four days to tell them that the president is still unable to carry out the rights and responsibilities of his job.

12 Then Congress will decide who will be president, meeting within forty-eight hours specifically for that reason if it's not already in session.

13 If Congress, within twenty-one days of receiving written notice, or, if not in session, within twenty-one days after it gathers, decides by a two-thirds vote of both houses that the president cannot carry out the rights and responsibilities of his job, the vice president continues to act as a substitute.

14 Otherwise, the president takes over the authority and responsibilities of the office again.

ORIGINAL TEXT

AMENDMENT XXVI
RATIFIED 7/1/1971

SECTION 1. The right of citizens of the United States, who are eighteen years of age or older, to vote, shall not be denied or abridged by the United States or by any state on account of age **1**.

SECTION 2. The Congress shall have power to enforce this article by appropriate legislation **2**.

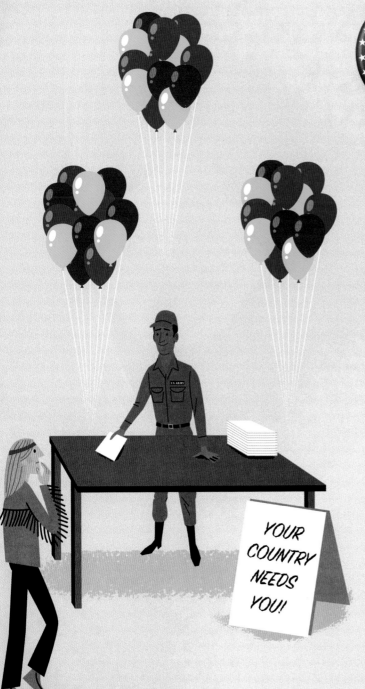

TRANSLATION

1 The voting rights of American citizens who are eighteen years or older will not be refused or limited by the federal or state governments because of the citizen's age.

2 Congress can write laws to make this happen.

DID YOU KNOW?

The 14th Amendment seems to assume that people under the age of twenty-one don't have a right to vote. While the Vietnam War was going on in the 1960s and 1970s, many people didn't think it was fair to say that someone was too young to vote—but old enough to fight in a war. (Men nineteen and older could be drafted to fight against their will; volunteers could join the military at eighteen, or seventeen with their parents' consent.) In 1970, Congress passed a law that made eighteen the age for voting in both national and state elections, but the Supreme Court ruled that the law didn't apply to the states. That meant that states had to keep track of who was old enough to vote in just federal elections (at age eighteen) and who was old enough to vote in state elections, too (at age twenty-one). Congress passed the 26th Amendment to fix the problem. Ratifying it would save the states a lot of trouble, and so they did that—in 107 days. It was the fastest an amendment has ever been ratified.

YOUR COUNTRY NEEDS YOU!

18 Today!

VOTE

ORIGINAL TEXT

AMENDMENT XXVII
RATIFIED 5/7/1992

No law, varying the compensation for the services of the Senators and Representatives, shall take effect, until an election of Representatives shall have intervened ❶.

LOOK BACK

In 1982, nineteen-year-old University of Texas student Gregory Watson learned that James Madison had proposed *twelve* amendments in 1789. Ten were ratified and became the Bill of Rights. Watson argued in a paper that the other two amendments were still alive because Madison hadn't included a date by which they had to be ratified. His teacher didn't buy it and gave him a C.

Watson was unhappy with his grade, so he wrote to state legislatures, trying to get them to ratify the amendments. When Congress voted itself a pay raise, people began to pay attention. In the next ten years, thirty-three more states ratified what became the 27th Amendment. Many of them hadn't been states when it was proposed. And thirty-five years after giving him a grade that inspired him to change the Constitution, Watson's teacher changed his grade to an A.

1 No law changing the pay of senators and representatives will start to apply until there's been another election for representatives.

DID YOU KNOW?

The 27th Amendment was ratified in 1992—but it was proposed in 1789. James Madison included it in the first twelve amendments he submitted to Congress. Ten others went on to become the Bill of Rights, but this one lingered for 203 years—the longest ratification time of any amendment.

JAMES MADISON

The Declaration of Independence

Delegates from the states to the Second Continental Congress met in Philadelphia in the spring of 1775, with the American Revolution already beginning. The Second Continental Congress directed the American war effort. It coordinated the state governments and functioned as a national government in the absence of any other body to do that job. It was the Second Continental Congress that appointed George Washington to lead the Continental Army in the fight against the British. And it was the Second Continental Congress that issued the Declaration of Independence, the document that explained why the new country was separating from Great Britain.

The Declaration of Independence is the first of three important documents written in the years of revolution and early nationhood. The second is the Articles of Confederation (see page 178), which set up the first formal American government. The third document, and by far the most important today, is the Constitution of the United States.

Note: *The following text is a transcription of the Stone engraving of the parchment Declaration of Independence. (The document is on display in the Rotunda at the National Archives Museum.) The spelling and punctuation reflect the original.*

In Congress, July 4, 1776.

The unanimous Declaration of the thirteen united States of America, When in the Course of human events, it becomes necessary for one people to dissolve the political bands which have connected them with another, and to assume among the powers of the earth, the separate and equal station to which the Laws of Nature and of Nature's God entitle them, a decent respect to the opinions of mankind requires that they should declare the causes which impel them to the separation.

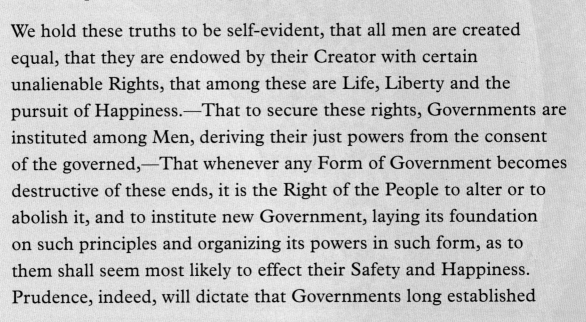

We hold these truths to be self-evident, that all men are created equal, that they are endowed by their Creator with certain unalienable Rights, that among these are Life, Liberty and the pursuit of Happiness.—That to secure these rights, Governments are instituted among Men, deriving their just powers from the consent of the governed,—That whenever any Form of Government becomes destructive of these ends, it is the Right of the People to alter or to abolish it, and to institute new Government, laying its foundation on such principles and organizing its powers in such form, as to them shall seem most likely to effect their Safety and Happiness. Prudence, indeed, will dictate that Governments long established should not be changed for light and transient causes; and accordingly all experience hath shewn, that mankind are more disposed to suffer, while evils are sufferable, than to right themselves by abolishing the forms to which they are accustomed. But when a long train of abuses and usurpations, pursuing invariably the same Object evinces a design to reduce them under absolute Despotism, it is their right, it is their duty, to throw off such Government, and to provide new Guards for their future security.—Such has been the patient sufferance of these Colonies; and such is now the necessity which constrains them to alter their former Systems of Government. The history of the present King of Great Britain is a history of repeated injuries and usurpations, all having in direct object the establishment of an absolute Tyranny over these States. To prove this, let Facts be submitted to a candid world.

He has refused his Assent to Laws, the most wholesome and necessary for the public good.

He has forbidden his Governors to pass Laws of immediate and pressing importance, unless suspended in their operation till his Assent should be obtained; and when so suspended, he has utterly neglected to attend to them.

He has refused to pass other Laws for the accommodation of large districts of people, unless those people would relinquish the right of Representation in the Legislature, a right inestimable to them and formidable to tyrants only.

He has called together legislative bodies at places unusual, uncomfortable, and distant from the depository of their public Records, for the sole purpose of fatiguing them into compliance with his measures.

He has dissolved Representative Houses repeatedly, for opposing with manly firmness his invasions on the rights of the people.

He has refused for a long time, after such dissolutions, to cause others to be elected; whereby the Legislative powers, incapable of Annihilation, have returned to the People at large for their exercise; the State remaining in the mean time exposed to all the dangers of invasion from without, and convulsions within.

He has endeavoured to prevent the population of these States; for that purpose obstructing the Laws for Naturalization of Foreigners; refusing to pass others to encourage their migrations hither, and raising the conditions of new Appropriations of Lands.

He has obstructed the Administration of Justice, by refusing his Assent to Laws for establishing Judiciary powers.

He has made Judges dependent on his Will alone, for the tenure of their offices, and the amount and payment of their salaries.

He has erected a multitude of New Offices, and sent hither swarms of Officers to harrass our people, and eat out their substance.

He has kept among us, in times of peace, Standing Armies without the Consent of our legislatures.

He has affected to render the Military independent of and superior to the Civil power.

He has combined with others to subject us to a jurisdiction foreign to our constitution, and unacknowledged by our laws; giving his Assent to their Acts of pretended Legislation:

For Quartering large bodies of armed troops among us:

For protecting them, by a mock Trial, from punishment for any Murders which they should commit on the Inhabitants of these States:

For cutting off our Trade with all parts of the world:

For imposing Taxes on us without our Consent:

For depriving us in many cases, of the benefits of Trial by Jury:

For transporting us beyond Seas to be tried for pretended offences

For abolishing the free System of English Laws in a neighbouring Province, establishing therein an Arbitrary government, and enlarging its Boundaries so as to render it at once an example and fit instrument for introducing the same absolute rule into these Colonies:

For taking away our Charters, abolishing our most valuable Laws, and altering fundamentally the Forms of our Governments:

For suspending our own Legislatures, and declaring themselves invested with power to legislate for us in all cases whatsoever.

He has abdicated Government here, by declaring us out of his Protection and waging War against us.

He has plundered our seas, ravaged our Coasts, burnt our towns, and destroyed the lives of our people.

He is at this time transporting large Armies of foreign Mercenaries to compleat the works of death, desolation and tyranny, already begun with circumstances of Cruelty & perfidy scarcely paralleled in the most barbarous ages, and totally unworthy the Head of a civilized nation.

He has constrained our fellow Citizens taken Captive on the high Seas to bear Arms against their Country, to become the executioners of their friends and Brethren, or to fall themselves by their Hands.

He has excited domestic insurrections amongst us, and has endeavoured to bring on the inhabitants of our frontiers, the merciless Indian Savages, whose known rule of warfare, is an undistinguished destruction of all ages, sexes and conditions.

In every stage of these Oppressions We have Petitioned for Redress in the most humble terms: Our repeated Petitions have been answered only by repeated injury. A Prince whose character is thus marked by every act which may define a Tyrant, is unfit to be the ruler of a free people.

Nor have We been wanting in attentions to our Brittish brethren. We have warned them from time to time of attempts by their legislature to extend an unwarrantable jurisdiction over us. We have reminded them of the circumstances of our emigration and settlement here. We have appealed to their native justice and magnanimity, and we have conjured them by the ties of our common kindred to disavow these usurpations, which, would inevitably interrupt our connections and correspondence. They too have been deaf to the voice of justice and of consanguinity. We must, therefore, acquiesce in the necessity, which denounces our Separation, and hold them, as we hold the rest of mankind, Enemies in War, in Peace Friends.

We, therefore, the Representatives of the united States of America, in General Congress, Assembled, appealing to the Supreme Judge of the world for the rectitude of our intentions, do, in the Name, and by Authority of the good People of these Colonies, solemnly publish and declare, That these United Colonies are, and of Right ought to be Free and Independent States; that they are Absolved from all Allegiance to the British Crown, and that all political connection between them and the State of Great Britain, is and ought to be totally dissolved; and that as Free and Independent States, they have full Power to levy War, conclude Peace, contract Alliances, establish Commerce, and to do all other Acts and Things which Independent States may of right do. And for the support of this Declaration, with a firm reliance on the protection of divine Providence, we mutually pledge to each other our Lives, our Fortunes and our sacred Honor.

The Articles of Confederation

Once it had adopted the Declaration of Independence, the Second Continental Congress needed to set up a national government. Delegates disagreed on a number of issues, however, and because the Revolutionary War was going on, their attention was divided. Finally, the delegates drew up the final version of the Articles of Confederation, which created a weak national government that was secondary to state governments. Soon after, in late 1777, the Continental Congress sent the Articles to the states to ratify.

In December 1777, Virginia became the first state to ratify the Articles. Other states signed on over the next few months, but the Articles required consent from every state to go into effect, and Maryland, Delaware, and New Jersey rejected them (although they were written by a delegate from Delaware, John Dickinson, who called the new country the "United States of America"). By early 1779, both New Jersey and Delaware had ratified the Articles, leaving Maryland as the lone holdout. Maryland finally signed on when the British raided its coast and the state turned to France for help—only to have the French minister suggest that it should ratify the Articles of Confederation first. So Maryland ratified the Articles in March 1781, providing the unanimous consent necessary for them to go into effect.

To all to whom these Presents shall come, we, the undersigned Delegates of the States affixed to our Names send greeting. Whereas the Delegates of the United States of America in Congress assembled did on the fifteenth day of November in the year of our Lord One Thousand Seven Hundred and Seventy seven, and in the Second Year of the Independence of America agree to certain articles of Confederation and perpetual Union between the States of Newhampshire, Massachusetts-bay, Rhodeisland and Providence Plantations, Connecticut, New York, New Jersey, Pennsylvania, Delaware, Maryland, Virginia, North Carolina, South Carolina, and Georgia in the Words following, viz. "Articles of Confederation and perpetual Union between the States of Newhampshire, Massachusetts-bay, Rhodeisland and Providence Plantations, Connecticut, New York, New Jersey, Pennsylvania, Delaware, Maryland, Virginia, North Carolina, South Carolina, and Georgia.

ARTICLE I. The Stile of this confederacy shall be, "The United States of America."

ARTICLE II. Each state retains its sovereignty, freedom and independence, and every Power, Jurisdiction and right, which is not by this confederation expressly delegated to the United States, in Congress assembled.

ARTICLE III. The said states hereby severally enter into a firm league of friendship with each other, for their common defence, the security of their Liberties, and their mutual and general welfare, binding themselves to assist each other, against all force offered to, or attacks made upon them, or any of them, on account of religion, sovereignty, trade, or any other pretence whatever.

ARTICLE IV. The better to secure and perpetuate mutual friendship and intercourse among the people of the different states in this union, the free inhabitants of each of these states, paupers, vagabonds and fugitives from Justice excepted, shall be entitled to all privileges and immunities of free citizens in the several states; and the people of each state shall have free ingress and regress to and from any other state, and shall enjoy therein all the privileges of trade and commerce, subject to the same duties, impositions and restrictions as the inhabitants thereof respectively, provided that such restrictions shall not extend so far as to prevent the removal of property imported into any state, to any other State of which the Owner is an inhabitant; provided also that no imposition, duties or restriction shall be laid by any state, on the property of the united states, or either of them.

If any Person guilty of, or charged with, treason, felony, or other high misdemeanor in any state, shall flee from Justice, and be found in any of the united states, he shall upon demand of the Governor or executive power of the state from which he fled, be delivered up, and removed to the state having jurisdiction of his offence.

Full faith and credit shall be given in each of these states to the records, acts and judicial proceedings of the courts and magistrates of every other state.

ARTICLE V. For the more convenient management of the general interests of the united states, delegates shall be annually appointed in such manner as the legislature of each state shall direct, to meet in Congress on the first

Monday in November, in every year, with a power reserved to each state to recall its delegates, or any of them, at any time within the year, and to send others in their stead, for the remainder of the Year.

No State shall be represented in Congress by less than two, nor by more than seven Members; and no person shall be capable of being delegate for more than three years, in any term of six years; nor shall any person, being a delegate, be capable of holding any office under the united states, for which he, or another for his benefit receives any salary, fees or emolument of any kind.

Each State shall maintain its own delegates in a meeting of the states, and while they act as members of the committee of the states.

In determining questions in the united states, in Congress assembled, each state shall have one vote.

Freedom of speech and debate in Congress shall not be impeached or questioned in any Court, or place out of Congress, and the members of congress shall be protected in their persons from arrests and imprisonments, during the time of their going to and from, and attendance on congress, except for treason, felony, or breach of the peace.

ARTICLE VI. No State, without the Consent of the united States, in congress assembled, shall send any embassy to, or receive any embassy from, or enter into any conferrence, agreement, alliance, or treaty, with any King prince or state; nor shall any person holding any office of profit or trust under the united states, or

Pennsylvania

any of them, accept of any present, emolument, office, or title of any kind whatever, from any king, prince, or foreign state; nor shall the united states, in congress assembled, or any of them, grant any title of nobility.

No two or more states shall enter into any treaty, confederation, or alliance whatever between them, without the consent of the united states, in congress assembled, specifying accurately the purposes for which the same is to be entered into, and how long it shall continue.

No State shall lay any imposts or duties, which may interfere with any stipulations in treaties, entered into by the united States in congress assembled, with any king, prince, or State, in pursuance of any treaties already proposed by congress, to the courts of France and Spain.

No vessels of war shall be kept up in time of peace, by any state, except such number only, as shall be deemed necessary by the united states, in congress assembled, for the defence of such state, or its trade; nor shall any body of forces be kept up, by any state, in time of peace, except such number only as, in the judgment of the united states, in congress assembled, shall be deemed requisite to garrison the forts necessary for the defence of such state; but every state shall always keep up a well regulated and disciplined militia, sufficiently armed and accounted, and shall provide and constantly have ready for use, in public stores, a due number of field pieces and tents, and a proper quantity of arms, ammunition, and camp equipage.

No State shall engage in any war without the consent of the united States in congress assembled, unless such State be actually invaded by enemies, or shall have received certain advice of a resolution being formed by some nation of Indians to invade such State, and the danger is so imminent as not to admit of a delay till the united states in congress assembled, can be consulted: nor shall any state grant commissions to any ships or vessels of war, nor letters of marque or reprisal, except it be after a declaration of war by the united states in congress assembled, and then only against the kingdom or State, and the subjects thereof, against which war has been so declared, and under such regulations as shall be established by the united states in congress assembled, unless such state be infested by pirates, in which case vessels of war may be fitted out for that occasion, and kept so long as the danger shall continue, or until the united states in congress assembled shall determine otherwise.

ARTICLE VII. When land forces are raised by any state, for the common defence, all officers of or under the rank of colonel, shall be appointed by the legislature of each state respectively by whom such forces shall be raised, or in such manner as such state shall direct, and all vacancies shall be filled up by the state which first made appointment.

ARTICLE VIII. All charges of war, and all other expenses that shall be incurred for the common defence or general welfare, and allowed by the united states in congress assembled, shall be defrayed out of a common treasury, which shall be supplied by the several states, in proportion to the value of all land within each state, granted to or surveyed for any Person, as such land and the buildings and improvements thereon shall be estimated, according to such mode as the united states,

in congress assembled, shall, from time to time, direct and appoint. The taxes for paying that proportion shall be laid and levied by the authority and direction of the legislatures of the several states within the time agreed upon by the united states in congress assembled.

ARTICLE IX. The united states, in congress assembled, shall have the sole and exclusive right and power of determining on peace and war, except in the cases mentioned in the sixth article—of sending and receiving ambassadors—entering into treaties and alliances, provided that no treaty of commerce shall be made, whereby the legislative power of the respective states shall be restrained from imposing such imposts and duties on foreigners, as their own people are subjected to, or from prohibiting the exportation or importation of any species of goods or commodities whatsoever—of establishing rules for deciding, in all cases, what captures on land or water shall be legal, and in what manner prizes taken by land or naval forces in the service of the united Sates, shall be divided or appropriated—of granting letters of marque and reprisal in times of peace—appointing courts for the trial of piracies and felonies committed on the high seas; and establishing courts; for receiving and determining finally appeals in all cases of captures; provided that no member of congress shall be appointed a judge of any of the said courts.

The united states, in congress assembled, shall also be the last resort on appeal, in all disputes and differences now subsisting, or that hereafter may arise between two or more states concerning boundary, jurisdiction, or any other cause whatever; which authority shall always be exercised in the manner following. Whenever the legislative or executive authority, or lawful agent of any state in controversy with another, shall present a petition to congress, stating the matter in question, and praying for a hearing, notice thereof shall be given, by order of congress, to the legislative or executive authority of the other state in controversy, and a day assigned for the appearance of the parties by their lawful agents, who shall then be directed to appoint, by joint consent, commissioners or judges to constitute a court for hearing and determining the matter in question: but if they cannot agree, congress shall name three persons out of each of the united states, and from the list of such persons each party shall alternately strike out one, the petitioners beginning, until the number shall be reduced to thirteen; and from that number not less than seven, nor more than nine names, as congress shall direct, shall, in the presence of congress, be drawn out by lot, and the persons whose names shall be so drawn, or any five of them, shall be commissioners or judges, to hear and finally determine the controversy, so always as a major part of the judges, who shall hear the cause, shall agree in the determination: and if either party shall neglect to attend at the day appointed, without showing reasons which congress shall judge sufficient, or being present, shall refuse to strike, the congress shall proceed to nominate three persons out of each State, and the secretary of congress shall strike in behalf of such party absent or refusing; and the judgment and sentence of the court, to be appointed in the manner before prescribed, shall be final and conclusive; and if any of the parties shall refuse to submit to the authority of such court, or to appear or defend their claim or cause, the court shall nevertheless proceed to pronounce sentence, or judgment, which shall in like manner be final and decisive; the judgment or sentence and other proceedings being in either case transmitted to congress, and lodged among the acts of congress, for the security of the parties concerned: provided that every commissioner, before he sits in judgment, shall take an oath to be administered by one of the judges of the supreme or superior court of the State where the cause shall be tried, "well and truly to hear and determine the matter in question, according to the best of his judgment, without favour, affection, or hope of reward": provided, also, that no State shall be deprived of territory for the benefit of the united states.

All controversies concerning the private right of soil claimed under different grants of two or more states, whose jurisdictions as they may respect such lands, and the states which passed such grants are adjusted, the said grants or either of them being at the same time claimed to have originated antecedent to such settlement of jurisdiction, shall, on the petition of either party to the congress of the united states, be finally determined, as near as may be, in the same manner as is before prescribed for deciding disputes respecting territorial jurisdiction between different states.

The united states, in congress assembled, shall also have the sole and exclusive right and power of regulating the alloy and value of coin struck by their own authority, or by that of the respective states—fixing the standard of weights and measures throughout the united states— regulating the trade and managing all affairs with the Indians, not members of any of the states; provided that the legislative right of any state, within its own limits, be not infringed or violated—establishing and regulating post-offices from one state to another, throughout all the united states, and exacting such postage on the papers passing through the same, as may be requisite to defray the expenses of the said office—appointing all officers of the land forces in the service of the united States, excepting regimental officers—appointing all the officers of the naval forces, and commissioning all officers whatever in the service of the united states; making rules for the government and regulation of the said land and naval forces, and directing their operations.

The united States, in congress assembled, shall have authority to appoint a committee, to sit in the recess of congress, to be denominated, "A Committee of the States," and to consist of one delegate from each State; and to appoint such other committees and civil officers as may be necessary for managing the general affairs of the united states under their direction—to appoint one of their number to preside; provided that no person be allowed to serve in the office of president more than one year in any term of three years; to ascertain the necessary sums of money to be raised for the service of the united states, and to appropriate and apply the same for defraying the public expenses; to borrow money or emit bills on the credit of the united states, transmitting every half year to the respective states an account of the sums of money so borrowed or emitted,—to build and equip a navy—to agree upon the number of land forces, and to make requisitions from each state for its quota, in proportion to the number of white inhabitants in such state, which requisition shall be binding; and thereupon the legislature of each state shall appoint the regimental officers, raise the men, and clothe, arm, and equip them, in a soldier-like manner, at the expense of the united states; and the officers and men so clothed, armed, and equipped, shall march to the place appointed, and within the time agreed on by the united states, in congress assembled;

but if the united states, in congress assembled, shall, on consideration of circumstances, judge proper that any state should not raise men, or should raise a smaller number than its quota, and that any other state should raise a greater number of men than the quota thereof, such extra number shall be raised, officered, clothed, armed, and equipped in the same manner as the quota of such state, unless the legislature of such state shall judge that such extra number cannot be safely spared out of the same, in which case they shall raise, officer, clothe, arm, and equip, as many of such extra number as they judge can be safely spared. And the officers and men so clothed, armed, and equipped, shall march to the place appointed, and within the time agreed on by the united states in congress assembled.

The united states, in congress assembled, shall never engage in a war, nor grant letters of marque and reprisal in time of peace, nor enter into any treaties or alliances, nor coin money, nor regulate the value thereof nor ascertain the sums and expenses necessary for the defence and welfare of the united states, or any of them, nor emit bills, nor borrow money on the credit of the united states, nor appropriate money, nor agree upon the number of vessels of war to be built or purchased, or the number of land or sea forces to be raised, nor appoint a commander in chief of the army or navy, unless nine states assent to the same, nor shall a question on any other point, except for adjourning from day to day, be determined, unless by the votes of a majority of the united states in congress assembled.

The congress of the united states shall have power to adjourn to any time within the year, and to any place within the united states, so that no period of adjournment be for a longer duration than the space of six Months, and shall publish the Journal of their proceedings monthly, except such parts thereof relating to treaties, alliances, or military operations, as in their judgment require secrecy; and the yeas and nays of the delegates of each State, on any question, shall be entered on the Journal, when it is desired by any delegate; and the delegates of a State, or any of them, at his or their request, shall be furnished with a transcript of the said Journal, except such parts as are above excepted, to lay before the legislatures of the several states.

ARTICLE X. The committee of the states, or any nine of them, shall be authorized to execute, in the recess of congress, such of the powers of congress as the united states, in congress assembled, by the consent of nine states, shall, from time to time, think expedient to vest them with; provided that no power be delegated to the said committee, for the exercise of which, by the articles of confederation, the voice of nine states, in the congress of the united states assembled, is requisite.

ARTICLE XI. Canada acceding to this confederation, and joining in the measures of the united states, shall be admitted into, and entitled to all the advantages of this union: but no other colony shall be admitted into the same, unless such admission be agreed to by nine states.

ARTICLE XII. All bills of credit emitted, monies borrowed, and debts contracted by or under the authority of congress, before the assembling of the united states, in pursuance of the present confederation, shall be deemed and considered as a charge against the united States, for payment and satisfaction whereof the said united states and the public faith are hereby solemnly pledged.

ARTICLE XIII. Every State shall abide by the determinations of the united states, in congress assembled, on all questions which by this confederation are submitted to them. And the Articles of this confederation shall be inviolably observed by every state, and the union shall be perpetual; nor shall any alteration at any time hereafter be made in any of them, unless such alteration be agreed to in a congress of the united states, and be afterwards con-firmed by the legislatures of every state.

And Whereas it hath pleased the Great Governor of the World to incline the hearts of the legislatures we respectively represent in congress, to approve of, and to authorize us to ratify the said articles of confederation and perpetual union, Know Ye, that we, the undersigned delegates, by virtue of the power and authority to us given for that purpose, do, by these presents, in the name and in behalf of our respective constituents, fully and entirely ratify and confirm each and every of the said articles of confederation and perpetual union, and all and singular the matters and things therein contained. And we do further solemnly plight and engage the faith of our respective constituents, that they shall abide by the determinations of the united states in congress assembled, on all questions, which by the said confederation are submitted to them. And that the articles thereof shall be inviolably observed by the states we respectively represent, and that the union shall be perpetual. In Witness whereof, we have hereunto set our hands, in Congress. Done at Philadelphia, in the State of Pennsylvania, the ninth Day of July, in the Year of our Lord one Thousand seven Hundred and Seventy eight, and in the third year of the Independence of America.

Vocabulary

ALLIANCE—an agreement to work together or be on the same side

AMBASSADORS—diplomats sent from one country to be the official representative in another country. Ambassadors conduct diplomacy and explain their government's views to the host country.

APPELLATE JURISDICTION—Most cases that reach the Supreme Court were heard first in a lower court and then appealed. The Supreme Court has "appellate jurisdiction" in cases that have to start in a lower court.

APPROPRIATION OF MONEY—money set aside for a purpose

ATTAINDER OF TREASON—having to give up rights and property after being convicted of treason

BAIL—letting a person charged with a crime stay out of jail until their trial, often after they leave money with the court to guarantee that they'll show up

BILL OF ATTAINDER—a law that declares someone guilty of a crime (instead of letting them have a trial and the chance to prove that they didn't commit the crime)

BILLS—written drafts of laws

BRIBERY—the act of offering or taking money or a favor in return for something

CHIEF JUSTICE—the head of the Supreme Court, who is the top-ranking judge in the country

CHUSE—choose (The Constitution has some spellings we don't use anymore—and also some random capitalization and typos!)

COMMANDER IN CHIEF—the person in charge of the country's military forces

COMMON LAW—The idea of common law comes from England, and it is called "common" because it's the same from place to place. It was based on custom and precedent—how cases of the same type had been decided before—rather than on written law. The United States borrowed some of its law from English common law.

CONFEDERATION—a loose organization in which the lower level (like states) has more power than the higher level (like the federal government)

CONGRESS—the lawmaking body, or legislature, which passes laws that apply to the whole country

CONSTITUTION—a document that establishes the basic principles of a government, how it will operate, and the rights of its citizens

CONSTITUTIONALLY INELIGIBLE—unable to become president because a person doesn't meet the requirements to be president listed in Article II of the Constitution

CONSULS—government officials who live in a foreign city and represent their own nation's interests there. They often help visitors from their nation with problems they have in the foreign country, such as paperwork or legal issues. A nation might send several consuls to another country, usually to large cities, but there is only one ambassador. Ambassadors outrank consuls.

CONVICTED—found guilty of doing something illegal (a crime)

CORRUPTION OF BLOOD—not letting a person pass property down to his or her children as part of the punishment for a crime

DEMOCRACY—a government run by the people, often through elected representatives

DIRECT TAXES—taxes on people or property rather than activities or transactions

DUTIES—taxes on things that are brought into the country or shipped out of it

ELECTORS—voters

EMOLUMENTS—money or items of value

ENUMERATION—a count, or census. A census counts the entire population of the country.

EX POST FACTO LAW—a law that makes something illegal and allows punishment of people who did it before the law made it illegal. Also a law that increases the punishment for a crime and applies the new punishment to people who committed the crime before the law was passed.

EXCISES—taxes on things made, sold, or consumed within the country

EXECUTE—to carry something out or perform a task; to do the job

EXECUTIVE DEPARTMENTS—agencies in the executive branch, such as the Department of the Treasury, Department of Agriculture, and Department of State. Heads of the executive departments are in the Cabinet, which advises the president.

FELONY—a serious crime. Felonies are sometimes violent and are bigger crimes than misdemeanors. A person convicted of a felony can go to jail for more than one year.

FORFEITURE—giving something up, like money or property, as a punishment

HE—The masculine pronoun is used in the Constitution, but the articles apply the same to a female president, lawmaker, or judge.

HIGH CRIMES AND MISDEMEANORS—This term can be understood in different ways. Serious crimes probably count, but the Framers were focused on misuse of government power.

HOUSE OF REPRESENTATIVES—the lower chamber, or part, of Congress, which has 435 members who are divided among the states based on their populations. Representatives serve shorter terms than senators. The House is the "lower" chamber because representatives have always been elected directly by the people. The Framers thought the House would be more connected to the people and their needs.

IMPARTIAL—fair; not favoring one side or the other

IMPEACHMENT—charging an official, like the president, the vice president, or a Supreme Court justice, with treason, bribery, or misuse of government power

IMPOSTS—taxes on imports (goods brought into the country)

INDENTURED SERVANTS—people who signed a contract to work for a set number of years in exchange for food and shelter, and sometimes for passage to America

INDICTMENT—an official charge that someone has committed a crime

JURY—a group of people who listen to evidence in a court case and decide if the person who's been charged is guilty or not guilty

LAW AND EQUITY—law and justice

LETTERS OF MARQUE AND REPRISAL—permission to act as a pirate. Nations that didn't have a big navy sometimes let private ships attack enemy ships, essentially letting them be pirates in the service of their country.

MAJORITY—more than half

MILITIA—an army that's called together when there's a threat. The United States didn't have a standing army (one that's always in place) at the time the Constitution was written. People were expected to leave their jobs when there was a war and join the army, then go home when the fighting was over.

MINISTERS—the people in charge of a government department (for example, the secretary of education)

NATURALIZATION—the process by which foreign-born people become citizens

NOBILITY—aristocracy. "Duchess," "countess," and "earl" are examples of noble titles.

OATH OR AFFIRMATION—An oath is a promise to tell the truth. An affirmation is saying that you'll tell the truth without swearing it. (Some people have religious objections to swearing an oath.)

OFFICERS OF THE UNITED STATES—federal officials with significant power

ORDER—instruction given by someone in charge; a command

ORIGINAL JURISDICTION—the authority of the Supreme Court to hear some cases directly, without those cases starting in a lower court. The Supreme Court has "original jurisdiction" in those cases.

PARDON—a cancellation of the punishment for a crime; forgiving the crime

PENSION—money that an employer pays its workers on a regular basis after they've retired

PIRACIES—attacks on and robberies of ships at sea

POLL TAX—money you have to pay to vote. Poll taxes were put in place to discourage voting by Black Americans, and sometimes poor Whites.

PRESIDENT PRO TEMPORE—a senator who is in charge of the Senate when the vice president of the United States isn't there

PRIMARY—an election to choose who will represent a political party in the general election. A primary election is between members of the same political party.

QUORUM—the minimum number of members who need to be present in the House or Senate so its work will be official

RATIFICATION—agreement to put a document into effect

REPEALED—overturned; canceled

REPRIEVE—putting off the punishment for a crime

REPUBLICAN FORM OF GOVERNMENT—a government in which ultimate power is held by the people and their elected representatives. A republic has an elected head rather than a hereditary king or queen.

RESOLUTION—a formal decision or proposal voted on by a legislature

REVENUE—income; for example, money coming to the government from people paying taxes

SENATE—the upper chamber, or part, of Congress. It is made up of one hundred senators—two from each state. Senators serve longer terms than members of the House of Representatives. The Senate is the "upper" chamber because originally senators were elected by state legislatures. The Framers thought this would distance senators from the people and provide stability to Congress.

STATE LEGISLATURE—the lawmaking body for a state, which can write laws affecting only that state

SUFFRAGE—the right to vote

TAXES—money paid to the government from people's wages and companies' profits. Taxes are also added to the cost of things that people buy.

TREASON—making war against the government or helping its enemies

TREATY—an official agreement between countries

TRIBUNAL—court

WRIT OF HABEAS CORPUS—a requirement that the government explain to a judge or court why someone was arrested and release them if the explanation isn't good enough

Suggestions for Further Reading

Barcella, Laura. *Know Your Rights! A Modern Kid's Guide to the American Constitution.* New York: Sterling Children's Books, 2018.

Baxter, Roberta. *The Magna Carta: Cornerstone of the Constitution* (Documenting U.S. History). Portsmouth, NH: Heinemann, 2012.

Catrow, David. *We the Kids: The Preamble to the Constitution of the United States.* New York: Puffin, 2005.

Cheney, Lynne V., and Greg Harlin. *We the People: The Story of Our Constitution.* New York: Simon & Schuster Books for Young Readers, 2012.

Demuth, Patricia, and Tim Foley. *What Is the Constitution?* New York: Penguin, 2018.

Fritz, Jean. *The Great Little Madison* (Unforgettable Americans). New York: Puffin Books, 1998.

Fritz, Jean, and Tomie dePaola. *Shh! We're Writing the Constitution.* New York: Puffin Books, 1997.

Hennessey, Jonathan, and Aaron McConnell. *The United States Constitution: A Graphic Adaptation.* New York: Hill and Wang, 2008.

Khan, Khizr. *This Is Our Constitution: What It Is and Why It Matters.* New York: Yearling Books, 2019.

Krull, Kathleen, and Anna DiVito. *A Kids' Guide to America's Bill of Rights.* New York: HarperCollins, 2015.

Maestro, Betsy, and Giulio Maestro. *A More Perfect Union: The Story of Our Constitution.* New York: HarperCollins, 2008.

Spier, Peter. *We the People: The Constitution of the United States of America.* Boston: Houghton Mifflin, 1997.

For Teachers

Monk, Linda R. *The Bill of Rights: A User's Guide.* Foreword by Justice Ruth Bader Ginsburg. New York: Hachette Books, 2018.

Monk, Linda R. *The Words We Live By: Your Annotated Guide to the Constitution.* New York: Hyperion Books, 2004.

About the Author
KATIE KENNEDY

Katie Kennedy has taught college history and American government for thirty years. She currently teaches in Iowa, where she lives with her husband and son. She once caught her then nine-year-old daughter sneak-reading the Constitution under the covers with a flashlight. She's never been prouder. She is the author of two young adult novels, *Learning to Swear in America* and *What Goes Up.*

About the Illustrator
BEN KIRCHNER

Ben Kirchner is an illustrator in Bath, England. He takes inspiration from midcentury illustration and loves to use detail and body language to develop characters on the page. He has worked for a wide range of publishing companies and news organizations, including the *Chicago Tribune*, the *New Yorker*, and the *Washington Post*.

About the Contributing Editor
KERMIT ROOSEVELT

Kermit Roosevelt teaches constitutional law at the University of Pennsylvania Law School. He is the author of two novels, *Allegiance* and *In the Shadow of the Law,* and a book about the Supreme Court, *The Myth of Judicial Activism.*

Index